**W9-BIO-938**

LIVING WITH STRANGERS IN THE U.S.A.
Communicating Beyond Culture

When you see the earth from the moon
you don't see any division there of
nations or states. This might be the
symbol for the new mythology to come.
That is the country that we are going
to be celebrating and those are the
people that we are one with.

Joseph Campbell
The Power of Myth

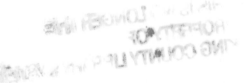

LIVING WITH STRANGERS IN THE U.S.A.

Communicating Beyond Culture

CAROL M. ARCHER

Language and Culture Center
University of Houston

Photographs by B. L. Striewski

REGENTS/PRENTICE HALL
Englewood Cliffs, New Jersey 07632

Library of Congress Cataloging-in-Publication Data

Archer, Carol M., (date)
  Living with strangers in the U.S.A. : communicating beyond culture
/ Carol M. Archer.
     p. cm.
  Includes bibliographical references.
  ISBN 0-13-538620-9 :
  1. English language—Textbooks for foreign speakers.
2. Communication—Social aspects—United States. 3. Readers—
Intercultural communication. 4. Intercultural communication.
5. Readers—United States. I. Title.
PE1128.A64 1991
428.6′ 4—dc20   90-40086
                                                      CIP

Editorial/production supervision
and interior design: **Shirley Hinkamp**
Cover design: **Diane Conner**
Pre-press buyer: **Ray Keating**
Manufacturing buyer: **Lori Bulwin**

 © 1991 by Prentice Hall Regents
Prentice-Hall, Inc.
A Simon & Schuster Company
Englewood Cliffs, New Jersey 07632

Printed in the United States of America
10 9 8 7 6 5 4

0-13-538620-9

Prentice-Hall International (UK) Limited, *London*
Prentice-Hall of Australia Pty. Limited, *Sydney*
Prentice-Hall Canada Inc., *Toronto*
Prentice-Hall Hispanoamericana, S.A., *Mexico*
Prentice-Hall of India Private Limited, *New Delhi*
Prentice-Hall of Japan, Inc., *Tokyo*
Simon & Schuster Asia Pte. Ltd., *Singapore*
Editora Prentice-Hall do Brasil, Ltda., *Rio de Janeiro*

**With loving gratitude to
my mother and my father
Lucy Mae Stokes Archer and Richard Isaac Archer**

Contents

Acknowledgments

The author wishes to acknowledge the support and encouragement received from her colleagues at the Language & Culture Center of the University of Houston during the writing of this textbook. In particular, she thanks Penny Cameron for her writing and publishing advice and Devi Spencer for her careful reading of and suggestions for the manuscript. To the many international friends and students whose lives form the basis for these stories, from Liliana Bassi to Maria and Kumar, thank you. A special thank you goes to Beryl Striewski for transforming the characters into the exquisite photographs in this book and to Lili Chen, Lien Nguyen, Samira Sharifi, Takao Kuwahara, Mohamad Al-Harbi, Maria Alejandra Hoyos, Alberto Antonio Travieso and Lee Parsons for gracing these pages with your presence. Finally, the author is particularly grateful to her father, Richard "Bud" Archer, who long ago opened the door to cross cultures for Laura Elberta, Billie Louise, Sarah Dean, Mary Elizabeth (who widened it), Carol Mae, and those who follow.

Introduction

The subject of this book is cross-cultural communication.This is the study of how to live with and communicate with people who are very different from oneself. Most of us have not read books about how to live with people from different cultures and even fewer of us have actually studied how to do this. We've simply stumbled through cross-cultural encounters, sometimes successful in our endeavors without really knowing how or why and sometimes "falling on our cultural faces." So studying cross-cultural communication skills may be a new experience—a course different from any that you may have had before. It focuses on how we normally act and think when we are with people from other cultures so that we better understand the communication process. Once we have this understanding, we can develop new skills and ways of thinking that make living with people who are very different not only easier but an exciting adventure in life. (1)

Overview of Cross-Cultural Communication

Cross-cultural communication, sometimes called intercultural communication, is a social science that is taught in colleges of social science or in communication departments. It is a relatively new field and has grown greatly since the early 1960s. It is applied in classes for international students studying in the United States or in companies which send employees to other countries to work or which have employees from a mixture of cultures working together. Most of the time, these individuals relate well and adapt to the new culture. However, there are always situations that present a problem. And in those situations, cross-cultural knowledge is very valuable. (2)

Communication

In this book, culture refers to the experience, knowledge, values, and behaviors of any one group of people. Communication is the process in which meaning is transmitted from one or more individuals to one or more other individuals. So cross-cultural communication is any communication which occurs between people with different cultural backgrounds. Note that these people do not necessarily have to be from different countries. For example, a Canadian and an American may find numerous areas of commonality in which they would not communicate cross culturally. (The term *American* in this text refers to the citizens of the United States, although the word *American* may also refer to the inhabitants of all the countries in North, South, and

Central America.) However, a Hopi Indian from Arizona talking with a middle-class Anglo (or American of Western European heritage) from New Jersey is communicating cross culturally, even though both are American. (3)

This book will teach you to look at your own culture, as well as the cultures of your classmates, in a new way, and to become aware of yourself and your classmates as being "products" of those cultures. You will also study cultural patterns that are very important in the United States, and by understanding these patterns you will better understand why Americans act and react as they do. (4)

In short, you will study the process of how to cross cultural boundaries with greater ease. You will study the problem expressed again and again by foreigners and Americans: "I understand your words, but I don't know what you mean." In this book, you will explore those deeper meanings; you will go beyond grammar and vocabulary to the values in each culture from which all communication—including language—springs. (5)

Overview of Reader

This is a reading textbook in which you will practice reading skills and develop your vocabulary. Each chapter is divided into two parts—a fictional section and an essay section. In the fictional section, certain vocabulary words are printed in boldface and are defined in context immediately following the story. Following the essay section is a vocabulary exercise which gives the definition to certain words used in the essay and you are to find the word that matches the definition. These words will be studied in exercises at the end of the reading. In addition, each reading section contains comprehension questions and suggested exercises based on the reading. (6)

Each chapter begins with the story of a fictional character who is studying in the United States. All together each of these fictional characters present the story of a "typical" semester in a university told from the point of view of students from all over the world. The book examines life in the United States from the perspective of fictional characters from eight different countries who study together in an American university. (7)

Areas of Emphasis

Three basic areas will be studied: (1) information about the nature of culture and the process of communication, (2) "culture bumps" or specific, personal experiences with individuals from other cultures, and (3) culture-specific information about the United States and other cultures. (8)

You will study these three basic areas by exploring them in the encounters of the fictionalized characters. Specific applications of theory will be examined in their exploits, then in your own experience. Later in the book you will study the dominant values and behavior patterns in American culture as they compare with other cultures. The book offers both traditional studies and experiential exercises. As a result of this, you will become much more aware of yourself as a "cultural being" as well as learning about other countries. (See pages xv and xvi at the end of this chapter for specific reading skill development suggestions). (9)

Course Objectives

Specifically, because each of you is living in a multicultural situation, this book will help you to live more effectively—to gain the greatest possible benefit from your interaction with people from other cultures. Foreign students will learn how to act in a particular situation in order to get the desired result. By learning new patterns of behavior, you do not become an American; rather you learn to choose the best pattern for attaining your objective in that particular situation. You may choose to behave in a way that you learned in your country and, if so, will learn what the consequences of retaining that behavior will be.

As a result, you can consciously choose new patterns at certain times, while retaining your own patterns at other times. Americans will become aware of the opportunities available in having hundreds of thousands of foreign students studying in American high schools and universities. You will discover the richness, perhaps for the first time, of living in a multicultural society. All will develop a new awareness of self and others that forms the basis for problem solving in the twenty-first century. (10)

Personal Objectives

Write as many goals for yourself as you wish.

At the end of this cross-cultural reading class, I will be able to

1.
2.
3.
4.
5.
6.
7.
8.
9.
10.

Course Objectives

At the end of the cross-cultural reading class, the students will be able to:

1. Identify cultural patterns in their own and other's behavior.
2. Distinguish between cultural and universal values—both for themselves and for others.
3. Identify major American cultural patterns and beliefs in individuals and in institutions.
4. Read English at a higher level.
5. Develop personal strategies for alleviating cultural misunderstanding and cultural conflict.

Comprehension Questions

Place a T in the blank for statements that are true and an F in the blank for statements that are false. Change the false statements so that they are true.

_____ 1. Cross-cultural communication is the study of how to live with and communicate with people who are different from oneself.

_____ 2. Cross-cultural communication is sometimes called intracultural communication.

_____ 3. Cross-cultural communication is a natural science.

_____ 4. Culture refers to the experience, knowledge, values, and behaviors of any one group of people.

_____ 5. Communication is the process in which meaning is translated from one or more individuals to one or more individuals.

_____ 6. Cross-cultural communication can only occur between peoples from different countries.

_____ 7. Culture bumps are general, impersonal experiences with individuals from other cultures.

_____ 8. You will study the dominant values and behavior patterns in American culture as they compare with those in other cultures.

_____ 9. Foreign students must use American patterns of behavior while living in the United States.

_____10. In this book, you will discover a new awareness of yourself.

Vocabulary Words

You can frequently guess the meaning of a word by reading the sentences around it. Find the paragraph in the essay on pages ix–xi with the same number as the number in the parentheses. Then find the word that fits the definition and write it in the blank.

Example:

(Paragraph 1) To do by chance, by accident _____ **stumbled** _____

(Paragraph 1) From one culture to another _____

(Paragraph 1) Abilities _____

(Paragraph 3) To pass on, to give _____

(Paragraph 5) Limits _____

(Paragraph 5) Comes from _____

(Paragraph 6) Not the truth _____

(Paragraph 7) Point of view _____

(Paragraph 9) Most important _____

(Paragraph 9) From experience _____

(Paragraph 10) Two or more cultures _____

(Paragraph 10) Result _____

(Paragraph 10) Keep_____

Vocabulary Exercise

Fill in the blanks with one of the vocabulary words on page xiii. The answers follow.

1. The _____ of driving too fast were that I got a speeding ticket.

2. The little boy _____ from behind the sofa to scare his sister.

3. Jean has a lot of _____ in painting pictures. She is very good.

4. Although he speaks both English and French, English is _____. He speaks it better than French.

5. Indonesia is a _____ country with people from many different cultures living together in harmony.

6. There are two ways to learn—from studying books (theoretically) or by living

   _____.

7. Without a passport, we cannot pass the _____ into Mexico.

8. I will _____ your message to our friend.

9. I prefer reading _____ stories rather than those that are true.

10. The two candidates disagree on taxes. Because of their different _____ they would choose opposite solutions.

1. consequences 2. sprang 3. skill 4. dominant 5. multicultural 6. experientially 7. boundary 8. transmit 9. fictional 10. perspectives

Word Forms

In English, an adverb can be formed by adding an -ly to the adjective form. In this exercise, choose the correct word form to fit into the following sentences. Write the part of speech at the end of each sentence (adjective or adverb).

Example:
skillful, skillfully

1. *He is a _____skillful_____ driver. (adjective)*

2. *He drives _____skillfully_____ . (adverb)*

cross-cultural, cross culturally

1. _____ communication is necessary for understanding. (   )

2. We communicate _____ very well. (   )

sentimental, sentimentally

1. I felt very _____ when I saw my old teacher. (   )

2. I reacted _____ when I saw my old teacher. (   )

multicultural, multiculturally

1. With students from all over the world, we have a _____ class. (   )

2. When students from different countries study together, they study

   _____. (   )

fictional, fictionally

1. All of his writing is _____. (   )

2. He writes _____. (   )

experiential, experientially

1. Her knowledge of the United States is _____. (   )

2. She has gained knowledge of the United States _____. (   )

Suggestions for Vocabulary Study

Write the vocabulary words that you do not know on 3 × 5 note cards. Write one word on each card. Carry the cards with you and in your spare moments (on the bus, during breaks) review the words. Write synonyms and phrases with the word in it. Do not write in your own language. Sketch pictures if it helps you to remember. Experiment to find what jogs your memory. Use different colors, sketches, numbers, and so on. You can exchange cards with classmates and "test" one another.

Buy packets of "stickies" (small pads of paper with glue on the back that enables you to attach the papers easily and quickly). Write vocabulary words that you are trying to learn and put them around your home or office. For example, place them on the wall next to the TV. During commercials, glance at them and repeat them. Experiment with different colors.

Write the words "in the air" with your finger. It helps to remember them.

Make a cassette tape of your voice saying the word and the definition and, perhaps, use the word in a sentence. Make a cassette for each chapter and listen to it for 15 to 30 minutes a day. If you jog or walk or do other exercise, that is an excellent time to listen to the words. Change the words on the cassette (or keep the cassettes and use them to review at mid-term and at the end of the semester).

Make it a point to use at least three new vocabulary words each day—even if you use them incorrectly!

Suggestions for Reading

Skimming—Skimming means to read through something very quickly—not reading it carefully. Try to skim an article before reading it.

Clustering—Train your eyes to read several words at a time rather than reading word by word. If you notice how you read in your own language, you probably read in groups. Have someone watch you read and tell you if you move your lips or head. If so, you are reading word by word. You need to practice reading two to four words at once. One way to practice is to take a plain piece of paper and, holding it on the page, move it quickly down the page, uncovering one line at a time and force your eyes to "bounce" across the lines, grabbing the meaning as they go. Move the paper more and more quickly until you are comfortable clustering. Practice this skill *every day*. Be careful. When your eyes begin to hurt, *stop* immediately. *Do not strain your eyes.*

Fictional writing is usually easier to read. Try reading it out loud to "feel" the rhythm of the language. Let the imagery of the writing carry you to the meaning. Read for pleasure. The more you read (no matter what!), the better you will read.

Expository writing sometimes requires different techniques. Often several readings may be necessary to understand difficult or conceptual material. If there are comprehension questions, read them before reading the article. They will frequently tell you what the author thinks is important to remember. Read paragraph headings and try to figure out the main ideas of the article. Look at photographs and see if they can help to explain the idea.

For more information about the field of cross-cultural communication:

HOOPES, DAVID S., PAUL B. PEDERSEN, and GEORGE W. RENWICK,   *Overview of Intercultural Education, Training and Research.* Washington, DC: Georgetown University, 1977. While the whole book has interesting articles about cross culture, the first and last articles deal specifically with the research and theories in cross-cultural communication.

HOOPES, DAVID S., and PAUL VENTURA,   *Intercultural Sourcebook.* LaGrange Park, IL: Intercultural Network, Inc. 1979. Presents specific training methodologies as well as an explanation of each method.

LIPPITT, GORDON L. and DAVID S. HOOPES, eds.,   *Helping Across Cultures.* Washington, DC and London, England: International Consultants Foundation, 1978. An excellent, short book that gives an overview of the field of cross-cultural communication and touches on the methods and techniques used in the field.

SEELYE, H. NED,   *Teaching Culture.* Lincolnwood, IL: National Textbook Company, 1984. A very readable book that approaches teaching culture a little differently than the other books in this bibliography.

WEEKS, WILLIAM H., PAUL B. PEDERSEN, and RICHARD W. BRISLIN,   *A Manual of Structured Experiences for Cross-Cultural Learning.* Washington, DC: Georgetown University, 1977. More specific exercises and methods for teaching and training in cross culture.

LIVING WITH STRANGERS IN THE U.S.A.

Communicating Beyond Culture

Chapter 1

Joy Taylor

The story begins when the teacher, Joy Taylor, goes into class on the first day of the semester. As she calls the roll, each student reminds her of former students and finally, she remembers her own overseas experience in Algeria. Notice how the story changes from the present tense to the past tense by the use of "flashbacks." As you read the story, think about why Joy has continued to teach for so many years.

Non-English Words that Appear in the Reading "Joy's Story"

Saigon (Ho Chi Minh City) – former capital of what was then called South Vietnam

Gran Mariscal – a scholarship program started in the 1970s in which the government of Venezuela sent thousands of students to the United States and other countries to study

arepas – a bread typical of Venezuela and neighboring countries that is made from corn meal

salsa – a type of music that is typical in Venezuela and other Latin countries

cuatro – a four-stringed musical instrument from Venezuela

costeña – a Spanish word meaning "someone from the coastal area"

haiik – a long, usually white scarf that covers the entire body worn by some women in Algeria

henna – a natural dye used by some women in the Middle East on their hair

JOY'S STORY

After so many years of teaching, Joy Taylor sometimes wondered why she continued. She was thinking along these lines as she walked to her cross-cultural communication class on the first day of the semester. This morning, as in previous semesters, she had picked up her class list and gone to the teacher's lounge. There with a cup of coffee, she went through the names—foreign and American.

In the classroom, she put her books on the table with an air of having been there many times. Now the list of names assumed form and shape in front of her. A knock on the door caught her attention, and a tall slender young man stepped inside.

"You'd think that after all this time that I'd be used to 'em wandering in late," **flashed** across Joy's mind as she motioned to a chair and said,

"Just have a seat,"

and in anticipation of his next question,

"anywhere."

She looked at the class list,

"Mr. Al-Ahmed, Abdul-Aziz?"

Her eye took in the tall, young man. After years of working with Middle Easterners, she mentally put him in a category labeled *Saudi, modernized.* She smiled slightly as she remembered other Saudis—polite, generous, intense in their relationships.

Her thoughts returned to the class. Light from the window **cast a shadow** on the face of the woman in the seat directly in front.

"Miss Vo?"

When Phi raised her head, her large dark eyes looked directly at Joy.

"Present."

I wonder what tales she could tell . . . and Joy recalled the many Vietnamese that had filled her composition class that April when *Saigon* fell and the young men and women had watched their families disappear on CBS evening news—then came to class to write essays while their hearts were breaking. Joy pulled her thoughts back to the list of names.

"Mr. Chavez?"

"Here."

His shirt open, he sprawled in his seat, his dark eyes laughing. Joy tried to repress a smile—The *Gran Mariscal*—how many Venezuelans had been in that huge scholarship program fueled by the oil of Venezuela. They'd hit the United States with parties, rapid fire Spanish, and *salsa*. And English language teachers across the nation learned about *arepas* and *cuatros*—in a hurry. Now it was a treat to find one in class.

"Mr. Nelson?"

"Here."

Joy looked at his open face. She smiled in anticipation of sharing her years of experience with this young Texan.

"Miss Lopez?"

"Here."

Looking into Luz Maria's dark eyes, Joy remembered the courtly Tomas, whom she had almost married—how long ago had it been?—14 years now. She reflected a moment on the richness of Colombian culture. But this one, I'll bet she's *costeña.*

"Which city are you from, Miss Lopez?"

"Cartagena."

"Nice city. Mr. Tanaka?"

With a small bow of his head, the slight man said,

"Present."

When she read the next name, she looked at the slender young woman who answered so softly, 'Zhu, Li Li.' Tall with a scarf around her hair, she sat easily in the chair and wore large glasses.

"Miss Al-Akhras?"

"Present."

Her *hennaed*, shoulder-length hair catching the light from the window, evoked visions for Joy of her trip into the Sahara desert. The memories of Algeria rushed back.

It was 18 years ago. She had only been in Algeria for a couple of weeks when one of her students, Fahti, invited her to visit her family in a small village deep in the Sahara. She had been delighted at the prospect of getting out of the capital where it seemed that nothing worked—at least on time. She left early in the morning with Fahti and her brothers, Mourad and Sherif. Her enthusiasm waned as they traveled hour after hour across the Sahara in unbelievable heat. Suddenly the unending road dropped precipitously. Spread below them was the dark green of an oasis, magnificent after the hours of desert browns and greys under the fierce sun. They wound their way down the side of the hill and moved slowly through the streets until they found a small hotel. After unpacking, the four decided to take a stroll in the early evening. They walked into the oasis where a donkey plodded slowly around and around an ancient water well just as donkeys had done for a millennium. Joy reflected on the centuries of human lives passing through this small oasis lasting for a season just as had the fallen palm leaves that crunched beneath her feet.

She was troubled by an incident that had happened that morning. A woman, veiled from head to toe, was walking beside the road. Joy had insisted that they stop the car so that she could take a photograph. The woman turned her head and raised her arm, and suddenly Joy realized that she had somehow insulted the human being under that white covering. Through the lens of her camera, the interesting photograph changed into a fellow human being. Joy felt vaguely ashamed.

In the streets again, she **gaped at** the shops with items hanging on every inch of wall and ceiling space, at the men in turbans and long skirt pants; they carefully avoided looking at her and at Fahti. She was still **incredulous** at the women in long *haiiks*. All at once, she was struck by the realization that people lived here in this **foreboding** environment, lived their lives, day by day, with no awareness of her reality. In fact, they were unaware that other realities existed. And at that moment, her reality of clocks and her mother and father in their frame home in Minnesota where her father was a high school principal, seemed like a dream. Joy felt very much like a stranger in a sea of foreigners.

That night, they decided to drive to the desert at the edge of the oasis town. The dark was so complete that she could feel its presence on her skin and the stars were huge. Joy stared at them until she felt herself disappear into **the void.**

As they drove back to town, the car was stopped by a wedding procession. One of the women invited Joy and Fahti to the women's party. They walked up a staircase—Joy holding tightly to Fahti's hand—and into a room that was filled with women and children. Fahti guided her round the groups of women sitting and praying on the floor and up to the bride, sitting on a straight chair waiting for her groom. She was dressed in red velvet with gold braid while layers of pearls **wound around** her neck. A small flower was painted on her cheek. She sat motionless. Joy felt very foreign and **awkward** and wanted only to get away from the noise and strange sounds of Arabic, the stares of the women, and the unfamiliar smells. Then she looked into the young bride's eyes and saw the same fear and excitement that she had seen in her sister Eileen's eyes on her wedding day last year.

Back in the hotel, she sat on the wide window sill and looked out onto the empty streets and listened to the drums from the wedding party. It seemed a year ago that she had left Algiers and a century ago that she had left Minnesota. Then she noticed that the drum beat **reverberated** in harmony with her heartbeat, and she felt a timeless kinship with those human beings that earlier had seemed so strange. How glad she had been to get away from Algiers and the frustration of trying to teach her students to be on time and to do things the American way. She had been feeling more and more uneasy as she reluctantly acknowledged her own **growing disdain** for Algerians and things Algerian. But tonight, she saw Algerians in a different light. And as she smelled the heavy desert air, she was moved by their common humanity and **staggered** by the difference between their lives and her own.

Her mind flashed with **insights.** As a teacher she wanted **to foster** acceptance and respect between peoples of the world. She realized that she had moved a step closer to doing this by finding a new perspective on her own world with today's journey. That was the difference between her and the Algerians in the village. She suddenly understood that every culture reflects a fundamental humanity, much as a prism reflects the sunlight. Each culture sparkles with special ways of living, with special ideas, and with special things which a "stranger"—if he or she knows how—can choose to add to his or her own special way of living and of thinking in a process that is sometimes uncomfortable and sometimes exhilarating.

Sitting on that window sill, Joy decided that the discomfort that she felt moving from her own world into another world was a small price to pay to discover new depths in herself and in others. **Weary** from the journey, she slept a deep and satisfying sleep.

And the class list continued—Henry Gambo, Cameroon; Luigi Saldri, Switzerland; Kathy Franklin, United States. . . .

"Good morning class. My name is Joy Taylor and this is Cross-Cultural Communication 1400. Welcome to a journey in cross-cultural learning. Look around you and discover your companions on this trip."

Vocabulary Words

1. **flash across one's mind**—think something quickly
2. **cast a shadow**—put a shadow
3. **sprawl in a seat**—sit in an informal and comfortable manner
4. **repress a smile**—not smile when one wants to
5. **courtly**—very polite
6. **slight**—small
7. **evoke visions**—bring images or memories to one's mind
8. **prospect**—opportunity
9. **wane**—grow less
10. **drop precipitously**—go down suddenly and at a sharp incline
11. **plod around**—walk slowly and heavily
12. **crunch**—make a crackling noise
13. **gape at**—stare at
14. **incredulous**—very surprised, almost unbelieving
15. **foreboding**—uncomfortable, unfriendly
16. **the void**—nothingness
17. **wound around**—go around and around
18. **awkward**—uncomfortable
19. **reverberate**—echo
20. **growing disdain**—a feeling of superiority that is increasing
21. **staggered by**—a feeling of extreme surprise
22. **insights**—surprising, instant realizations
23. **foster**—encourage, to create
24. **weary**—tired

Discussion Questions

In small groups, discuss the following questions. Be prepared to share your discussion with the class.

1. What does the author mean by "insights"? Describe several insights that she experienced. Why are insights important in learning cross-cultural communication?

2. What does the author mean by "every culture reflects a fundamental humanity?" Do you agree? Why or why not?

3. What are special ways of living and meaning that your culture could offer to the world? What are special ways of living and meaning that American culture could offer to the world?

4. Why do you suppose that Joy continues to teach?

THE JOY OF CULTURE

Culture

Culture—how would we human beings live without our multitude of cultures? Indeed what would our life be like if suddenly our culture were to disappear? We would be bereft of speech, of gesture, of protection from the environment, and furthermore, we could not evaluate any sight, sound, smell, or any sensation whatsoever. In order to understand the impact of this supposition, we have only to recall the definition of culture in the introduction as "experience, knowledge, values, and behavior of any one group of people." This simple definition, when examined, reveals layer upon layer of life's patterns. To have a sense of the profundity of this statement, you have only to think for a moment of the groups of people with whom you share a history, a knowledge. (1)

Cultural Values

The values of a people are those things that are considered to be important. These include beliefs, religion, and ideas that we normally never question. Behaviors include speaking, rituals, and patterns of living. As you can see, there is very little in our lives that is not influenced by the culture in which we are raised. And for the most part, all of these things are so integral a part of our lives that we are completely unaware of this enormous influence. (2)

Ethnocentrism

Ethnocentrism is the largely unconscious belief that one's own way of doing things, one's own beliefs and way of life is the correct way or is the "normal" way of living. Everybody is ethnocentric about his or her culture and is unaware of the ethnocentrism. It is only when our behavior or values are placed in juxtaposition with another's that we become aware. And then, too frequently, we become aware only of "their culture" while we ourselves remain "normal." We can see an example of ethnocentrism in Joy's perceptions of Algerians. She sees them as being unable to do things "the American way" and judges them to be inferior as a result. (3)

In order to be effective in communicating cross culturally, we must be able to recognize our own cultural being. And to recognize ourselves as cultural beings is as difficult as it is for the bird to recognize the air or the fish to recognize the water. Yet that is precisely the task facing us in today's world. To meet this task, we must recognize that culture shapes the way in which we perceive reality. Joy began the process of recognizing herself as a cultural being on the trip into the Sahara. She realized that the Algerians' reality was as absolute for them as hers was for her, and she began to question her own perceptions. (4)

Perceptions

Since each person is simultaneously an individual, a member of a family, and a member of a culture at large, no event—even if viewed by twin brothers—would be perceived in exactly the same way. Once individuals are from different cultures, the possibility of completely different perceptions of the same event increases a hundredfold. Let us look for a moment at exactly what happens in the perception of an event. (5)

1. Occurrence of the event
2. Physiological impact
3. Organization
4. Evaluation
5. Reaction

Culture (as well as the other two factors previously mentioned) impacts on each of these steps.

1. The fact that we choose one event over another is culturally determined. Our culture teaches us to distinguish between noise and information, to pay attention to this and to ignore that. When an individual goes into a new culture, there are many things that people in that culture "see" that the newcomer does not. Yet the newcomer will notice things that the people there do not.
2. Sensory response to events has been shown to be partially culturally determined. For example, Japanese and Americans have differing abilities to hear certain sounds.

3. Language, being a categorizing system, determines how an event is organized. For example, *gordo* in Spanish can be a nickname while its translation in English, *fat,* is usually an insult when applied to an individual.
4. It is primarily our culture that teaches us the criteria we have for determining that which is good, bad, beautiful, ugly, respectful, and so on.
5. It is again primarily our culture that teaches the various appropriate responses that we have for responding to any given situation that we confront in life. (6)

Descriptive and Judgmental Observations

We can use Joy's experience to begin to understand the process of how human beings develop cultural perceptions of one another. A critically important step in cross-cultural encounters is to develop the ability to distinguish between an observation and the resulting assumption or opinion. While it is somewhat artificial, it is useful to label these as descriptive observations and judgmental observations. A descriptive observation is one in which the event is described with no interpretation added (a report of exactly what happened), while a judgmental observation reflects the viewpoint of the observer. One way of testing whether or not an observation is judgmental is to ask the question, "Would I know that without being inside the head or heart of the other person?" If the answer is yes, then the observation is descriptive; if the answer is no, then the observation is judgmental. If Joy describes the Algerian women wearing *haiiks* as second-class citizens or as being repressed, that is a judgmental observation. If she says the women wear a long, white piece of cloth that covers them from the top of their head to the top of their ankles, then she has made a descriptive observation. This ability to separate is more easily said than done. A great deal of practice and self-motivation is required to become proficient. (7)

Culture permeates our perceptual processes, at the same time providing us with valuable information for living in our own culture and frequently providing us with invalid and/or insufficient information for living in a foreign culture. (8)

Comprehension Questions

Place a T in the blank for statements that are true and an F in the blank for statements that are false. Change the false statements so that they are true.

_____ 1. Culture includes experience, knowledge, values, and behavior of any one group of people.

_____ 2. Language and religion are separate from culture.

_____ 3. Ethnocentrism is the belief that one's culture is the same as others.

_____ 4. There is no great need in today's world to recognize one's own culture.

_____ 5. Judgmental observations are always accurate.

_____ 6. Descriptive observations describe exactly what happened.

_____ 7. It is easy to separate descriptive from judgmental observations.

_____ 8. Twin brothers see things in exactly the same way.

_____ 9. Culture teaches us to distinguish one event over another.

_____ 10. There are no cultural differences between sensory perceptions.

Vocabulary Words

You can frequently guess the meaning of a word by reading the sentences around it. Find the paragraph in the essay on pages 6–8 with the same number as the number in the parentheses. Then find the word that fits the definition and write it in the blank.

Example:

(Paragraph 1) A large number, many _____ *multitude* _____

(Paragraph 1) To be without _____

(Paragraph 1) Educated guess, belief _____

(Paragraph 1) Depth, importance _____

(Paragraph 2) Necessary, important _____

(Paragraph 2) Big, huge _____

(Paragraph 3) Side by side, in comparison _____

(Paragraph 4) Job, work _____

(Paragraph 6) Influences _____

(Paragraph 6) Short name _____

(Paragraph 7) Educated guess, belief _____

(Paragraph 7) Able to do something well _____

(Paragraph 8) Spreads or passes through _____

Vocabulary Exercise

Fill in the blanks with one of the following vocabulary words listed on pages 5 and 9. The answers follow.

1. I ran for 12 miles, came home and went to bed because I felt very _____.

2. He made a very _____ bow of his head and said hello.

3. I have an _____ diamond ring. It is huge.

4. The _____ for William is Willie.

5. The _____ of cleaning the car is my responsibility. It is my favorite job.

6. The leaves _____ when we drove the car over them. It was a wonderful sound.

7. Looking at old photographs always _____ memories of my past. The memories come back every time.

8. When I fry eggplant, the oil _____ the slices of eggplant.

9. Reading my old diary gave me some _____ into my problem.

10. The policeman looked at my license and told me that it was _____ and gave me a ticket for an expired license.

1. weary 2. slight 3. enormous 4. nickname 5. task 6. crunched 7. evokes 8. permeates 9. insights 10. invalid

Word Forms

In English, a noun can be formed by adding a suffix to the verb form. A common suffix is -tion. Choose the correct word form to fit into the following sentences. Write the part of speech at the end of each sentence (noun, verb).

Example:
to suppose, supposition

1. *I _____suppose_____ that she went to New York. (verb)*

2. *I have the _____supposition_____ that she went to New York. (noun)*

to integrate, integration

1. The _____ of culture and language is complete. (   )

2. The language student must _____ his study of language with a study of the culture. (   )

to assume, assumption

1. He _____ that the test would be on Friday. (   )

2. He had the _____ that the test would be on Friday. (   )

to permeate, permeation

1. The _____ of the sand with water was total. (   )

2. The water _____ the beach at high tide. (   )

to invalidate, invalidation

1. Losing the picture _____ the passport. (   )

2. The _____ of the passport was caused by losing the picture. (   )

Exercises

1. List as many groups as possible with whom you share a history, experience, knowledge, values, and behavior.

2. Place a J by the following statements that are judgmental observations and a D by those that are descriptive statements. Write an interpretation that is possible after those that are descriptive. In small groups, check one another's work.

_____ a. Americans do not have strong family ties.
_____ b. Many American children leave home at around age 18.
_____ c. She's a very good teacher.
_____ d. People drive crazy in this city.
_____ e. American students do not respect their teachers.
_____ f. She's crying.
_____ g. His eyes are closed, his forehead wrinkled, his mouth open, his head inclined to the left and he is saying, "Help."
_____ h. They are sad.

____ i. I have too much homework tonight.

____ j. His hand is in her mouth.

3. Cut out a newspaper article and underline only the descriptive observations.

FOR MORE INFORMATION ABOUT CULTURE AND LANGUAGE LEARNING:

BENEDICT, RUTH,   *Patterns of Culture.* Boston: Houghton Mifflin Company, 1934. **Describes three societies as well as dealing in the first chapter with cultural blindness and race prejudice.**

COLE, MICHAEL and SYLVIA SCRIBNER,   *Culture and Thought: A Psychological Introduction.* New York: John Wiley & Sons, Inc., 1974. **The first chapter deals with culture and cognition and Chapters 4 and 5 deal in depth with the relationship between culture and perception.**

SAMOVAR, LARRY A. and RICHARD E. PORTER,   *Intercultural Communication: A Reader.* Belmont, CA: Wadsworth Publishing Company, Inc., 1972. **An anthology that has long been the foundation for cross-cultural communication.**

VALDES, JOYCE M.,   *Culture Bound: Bridging the Cultural Gap in Language Teaching.* Cambridge, England/New York: Cambridge University Press, 1986. **Comprehensive anthology that includes theory and application of cross-cultural ideas.**

FOR MORE INFORMATION ABOUT AMERICAN CULTURE:

COMMAGER, HENRY STEELE,   *The American Mind.* New Haven, CT: Yale University Press, 1950.

GARRETSON, LUCY R.,   *American Culture: An Anthropological Perspective.* Dubuque, IA: Wm. C. Brown Company Publishers, 1976. **Includes American attitudes about nature, rationality, home, school and work. Easy to read.**

STEINBECK, JOHN,   *America and Americans.* New York: Viking Penguin, Inc. 1966. **A classic American author on Americans.**

YANKELOVICH, DANIEL,   *New Rules: Searching for Self-Fulfillment in a World Turned Upside Down.* New York: Random House, 1981.

Chapter 2

Li Li

The story continues as we read a series of letters that Li Li, the Chinese student in Joy's class, writes to her grandmother about her first semester at the university in the United States. As you read the story, notice the relationship between the dates of the letters and Li Li's emotions. Do you think most people experience a similar adjustment when they move to a new country?

Non-English Words that Appear in the Reading "Li Li: PRC"

juhua – a flower, chrysanthemum
jiao-zi – a small pie, filled with meat or vegetables
Lao Tai Tai – grandmother, a term of respect used with older women in Chinese culture

LI LI: PEOPLE'S REPUBLIC OF CHINA

Li Li stretched her long legs under the student desk and leaned back in the straight chair in her dorm room. She closed her eyes and remembered leaning on the concrete double sink in their apartment in Shanghai watching Grandmother transplant a yellow *juhua* from one pot to another. She breathes deeply and smells the water in the soil and sees again the sun on her grandmother's wrinkled hands as Grandmother's words ring in her ears:

> Granddaughter. When I was a young girl and came to Shanghai from Hunan Province, I was like this flower, young and strong. But when I moved to Shanghai, like a transplanted flower, I felt weak and confused. You, too, will pass through this time in America. You must be strong and remember your roots. Remember to treat yourself well during the time of transplantation.

Then Li Li's mind raced back to Shanghai airport where she, fighting back tears, is saying goodbye to her grandmother, family, and friends, when one of her bulging suitcases pops open, spilling clothes and foodstuff all over the floor. Everyone scrambles as airline officials begin hustling people on board.

Li Li straightens up and brings her mind back to the task at hand. She picks up a pen to begin the letter. Memories of the last two weeks roll through her mind like a montage

Seeing the skyline of the city for the first time.
Moving her suitcases into the university dorm room.
Walking across campus with the sun shining one moment then a sudden autumn shower and the nice American student sharing his umbrella with her.
And the ever-present hot water at the touch of her hand.

September 6

Dear Grandmother:

I'm not like your transplanted flower after all. I love it in America and everyone is wonderful with me. I have a really nice roommate, Gabriela, who is from Mexico and has been here for three years already. She is very kind and helpful to me. We share many things. We often sit up late at night talking. She introduces me to her friends and teaches me how to work all the marvelous machines here in America. Oh

Grandmother, Americans do everything with machines. Can you imagine—they get coffee, food—even money from a machine. And they are so friendly they smile at you even when they don't know you. Strangers at bus stops talk to one another about personal things like what you're studying or what year you are in school. I like my classes very much—especially my cross-cultural communication class. In that class my classmates are from all over the world. There is Luz Maria from Colombia, Phi from Vietnam, Abdul Aziz from Saudi Arabia, Najwa from Syria and Americans. Najwa, Luz Maria, Phi, and I have lunch together and practice our English every day. And Brian, an American boy in the class, sometimes eats with us and helps us. My cross-cultural teacher, Miss Joy, is very nice and always helps us and gives us advice. And this is a most beautiful city with lots of new things to try out and places to visit. And everything is so modern and new—so unlike China with its centuries of traditions that we keep just as our fathers and grandfathers did. So you see Grandmother, I am a strong flower and have no problems in being transplanted.

Your granddaughter, Li Li

Time passes

Li Li sits looking out a window. People walking by are **reflected** in the glass. A tear rolls down her cheek. She sighs and picks up a pen to write.

In Shanghai, Grandmother sits by a window, where the flower that she transplanted is looking a bit **bedraggled**. The leaves are yellow and the blossoms are brown around the edges.

September 30

Dear Grandmother:

Oh dear, I have spoken too **hastily**. Gabriela says that what I have is called "culture shock." All I know is that my heart is breaking. I think of you and Mother and my friends all the time. I'm always looking at my watch and counting on my fingers to see what time it is back in China and imagining what you and Mother and Father are doing at that very moment. I feel like I'm living with one foot in America and the other foot in China. I always carry the photo of all of us in front of the Great Wall **tucked** in my book. Even in class, my mind is back in China. I was so embarrassed yesterday when the teacher caught me writing a letter to Mother during class. It seems that things got worse right after I wrote the last letter. Gabriela and Brian are now too busy with their other classes to spend much time with us—everybody is so busy. I live for letters from home. I rush to the **mailbox** immediately after class and my heart breaks if it is empty but my whole evening is golden if I find that brown airmail envelope inside. I keep all the letters and read them over and over again. And I'm losing weight—the food here has no taste. How I would love to have some of your *jiao-zi* right now. And I'm sleeping much more; I can't seem to get started. And I'm worried about my studies. Grandmother, I just can't seem to concentrate. In China I could easily study for 4 or 5 hours **straight**, but here I read a sentence and then my mind just wanders off and I have to start over again and again. I just have no desire to go anywhere or do anything. Time just pushes me here and there and my money is going so fast. Everything costs money here! I'm so surprised at how much everything costs. There are so many things to learn—not just English language but how to take the bus, how to wash clothes, and a thousand other things and I make so many mistakes. I don't know if I'll ever be able to live here comfortably.

I miss you so much.

Li Li

Time passes

Grandmother is at the door waiting for the **postman**. He approaches and says, "Hello, *Lao Tai Tai*."
"Hello. Do you have any letters for me?"
He laughs,
"Yes, here it is."
Grandmother takes the letter in her wrinkled, old hands. The transplanted flower behind her has now **recuperated** somewhat.

October 14

My Dear Grandmother:

I am feeling much better than I did in my last letter to you. One thing that helped a lot was that one night Gabriela and I sat and talked for a long time and I told her how I felt. She told me that she went through the same thing and that I was just fine. She suggested that I do some physical exercise and make an effort to get out and meet people. And now in class, Miss Joy is teaching us a lot about American culture and I'm beginning to understand a little about why they act the way they do. And I guess time helps. One day, it just seemed like I was better. I still miss you and everyone else but I feel like I'm going to be o.k. now. People know me and I know quite a few people also. I feel like the university is home now and I can study better, though still not as good as in China but Gabriela says that will come later. And even though I don't know everything about American life, I know some things and now I know how to learn more.

Your happier granddaughter,

Li Li

Time passes

Li Li, looking at a calendar, marks off September and October. She sighs, takes a pen and begins to write.

November 20

Honorable Grandmother:

I'm afraid I made a serious mistake in coming here. After all back home, I had a good job and now everyone will be ahead of me. To tell you the truth, I can't remember now why I thought it would be so great to come to America to study. And the Americans, now that I know them better, I discover that I don't like them very much at all. In fact, the longer I am here the more proud I am to be Chinese. It's easier to be with other Chinese. We understand one another. The other Chinese told me I was just a baby chick and would soon find out about the Americans. And they were right—they are only interested in themselves and in making money. They are very impolite. I even see boys and girls **entwined** in one another's arms in public. And they're not as advanced as we have been told. The professors don't know how to teach at all. They're more interested in being our friends than in teaching. Although, sometimes, I wonder what I'm missing.

Your disappointed granddaughter,

Li Li

As Li Li walks to the post office, she is approached by an obviously new, obviously lost American student.

"Excuse me. Could you tell me where the dorm office is?"

Li Li hesitates a moment, then looks at her face and smiles.

"Sure. It's over there. Listen, it's on my way. I'll walk with you. Are you a new student?"

The two girls walk away, the new student relieved and smiling.

Time passes

January 9

Dear Grandmother:

The new semester has started. I'm in the same dorm room and am very happy that Gabriela and I are roommates again. I'm also helping new students to adjust, I give them a tour of the campus and show them which books to buy. It seems strange to think that only a few months ago I was like them. I feel like I have come very far in a short time. Last night I cooked Chinese food for some of my old classmates—Najwa, Brian and Luz Maria. I think that we will always have a special relationship with one another. I think, Grandmother, that I have finally arrived in America. I have not lost my Chinese roots. In fact, they're stronger than ever.

Respectfully, your granddaughter,

Li Li

Grandmother takes off her glasses, folds the letter, and puts it back into the envelope. She then places the envelope under the flower pot—a flower pot filled with huge blossoms, resplendent in the sunlight.

Vocabulary Words

1. **concrete**—artificial stone made by mixing sand and gravel
2. **sink**—a container into which water runs
3. **soil**—dirt
4. **wrinkled**—skin that is not smooth because of small folds that come with age

5. **transplantation**—to remove and plant in another place
6. **fighting back tears**—trying not to cry
7. **bulging**—so full that it swells out
8. **scrambled**—ran in every direction quickly
9. **montage**—series of pictures
10. **shower**—rain
11. **reflected**—pictured as in a mirror
12. **bedraggled**—looking dirty and beat up
13. **hastily**—quickly
14. **tucked**—to put something where it will be safe
15. **mailbox**—small box where one receives letters
16. **straight**—continuously
17. **postman**—mailman
18. **recuperated**—got better
19. **entwined**—wrapped around

Discussion Questions

In small groups, discuss the following questions. Be prepared to share your discussion with the class.

1. Why did Grandmother tell Li Li to take care of herself during the time of transplantation? What kind of advice did people give you before you left your country?

2. In Li Li's second letter, she says she has culture shock. What do you think she meant by that? Have you experienced culture shock?

3. In Li Li's last letter, she says that she has finally arrived in America. What do you suppose she meant by that?

LETTERS FROM LI LI

Cultural Adjustment Cycle

When someone leaves his or her country and goes to live in a new one, that person is like a flower being transplanted. And just as the flower needs special care and time to adjust to the new flower pot, so does the foreigner in a new land. It is during this time that the individual has strong reactions to what L. Robert Kohls calls "the psychological disorientation" in his book, *Survival Kit for Overseas Living*. He or she can experience intense discomfort, irritability, bitterness, resentment, homesickness, depression, or physical illness. While everyone has a cultural adjustment period, not everyone experiences it to the same degree. Some people have a brief adjustment period and they barely notice going through it. Other people have a much more pronounced adjustment period. The adjustment cycle forms a W curve with a high point at the beginning, then a sinking followed by another high point, then a second low point and finally a high that signals adjustment to the new culture. (1)

We can trace Li Li's adjustment by reading her letters to her grandmother. The first one reflects her excitement at being in America. The second **chronicles** her descent into culture shock. The third shows her initial adjustment and the fourth expresses her mental isolation. By the fifth letter, she has begun to be fully integrated into the society and, like Grandmother's flower, is blossoming. (2)

Culture Shock

Kohls cautions that culture shock should not be confused with frustration which has a specific cause. Rather culture shock is a general condition which comes from being in an environment which threatens your total belief system. It is cumulative and builds up slowly (Kohls, 1979). (3)

Kohls says that culture shock results from being cut off from cultural cues, especially those subtle, indirect ways you have for expressing feelings. It comes from living and working in ambiguity, from having your own values brought into question, from being put in a situation in which you are expected to perform at maximum speed and efficiency but in which the rules have not been adequately explained. This is, perhaps, best expressed by Kalvero Oberg, the man who first diagnosed culture shock.

> These signs and clues include the thousand and one ways in which we orient ourselves to the situations of daily life: When to shake hands and what to say when we meet people, when and how to give tips, how to give orders to servants, how to make purchases, when to accept and when to refuse invitations, when to take statements seriously and when not. . . . (Kohls, 1979). (4)

The Adjustment Process in a New Culture*

The W curve of the adjustment process can be diagrammed as follows:

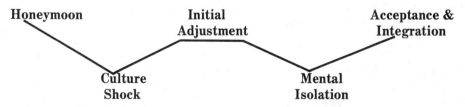

*Deena Levine and Mara Adelman, *Beyond Language,* pp. 198-199. Prentice Hall, Inc., Englewood Cliffs, New Jersey, 1982. (5)

A similar process occurs when the individual returns to his or her own culture. (5)

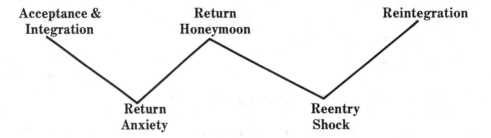

Some Characteristics of Each of the Stages

HONEYMOON

1. Feelings of a dream come true
2. Everything is new and exciting—a new adventure
3. Frequently, people help the "new arrival" out (6)

CULTURE SHOCK

1. Physical
   a. Stomach or bowel upset
   b. Tiredness, inability to concentrate
   c. Change in sleep patterns; sleep more or less than back home
   d. Change in eating habits—no appetite, or eating more than usual (7)
2. Psychological
   a. Thinking of what people back home are doing at this hour; living with a foot in each culture
   b. Extreme homesickness; grief
   c. Fear of being able to succeed, to perform
   d. Dreaming each night of "back home" and waking to the new culture with disappointment (8)

INITIAL ADJUSTMENT

1. Feeling of hopefulness, ability to perform well
2. Recognition that one has a "role," a place in the new culture
3. Although still missing "back home," feeling somewhat "connected" to people in new culture
4. Feelings of relief and new self-confidence (9)

MENTAL ISOLATION

1. Feelings of disdain and anger against the host culture
2. Feelings of self-doubt and worry that people back home are passing one by
3. Resentment over loss of status
4. Disappointment in oneself and/or the host culture (10)

ACCEPTANCE AND INTEGRATION

1. Stop trying to change host culture or making constant comparison to one's own culture
2. Develop strategies for living day to day (11)

RETURN ANXIETY

1. Sudden awareness of leaving host country "forever"
2. Sadness at leaving friends
3. Fear of ability to "fit back in" one's home country (12)

RETURN HONEYMOON

1. Extreme happiness upon return
2. Everyone listens to one's experiences and is interested (13)

REENTRY SHOCK

1. Same as culture shock with the difference that there is a feeling of alienation since there is no one back home with whom one can share these feelings.
2. Also a feeling of betrayal since these feelings are unexpected in one's "native" culture. Usually feelings of anger toward oneself and/or one's culture. (14)

REINTEGRATION

1. Occurs when one has found a way to validate one's overseas experience. (15)

Comprehension Questions

Put an F by those statements that are false and a T by those that are true. Rewrite the false statements so that they are true.

_____ 1. Not everyone has a cultural adjustment period.
_____ 2. Everyone has exactly the same experience as they go through the cultural adjustment period.
_____ 3. Culture shock is caused by a specific problem.
_____ 4. Kalvero Oberg is the first person to diagnose culture shock.
_____ 5. When someone returns to his or her own country, he or she also passes through a cultural adjustment cycle.
_____ 6. If someone is dreaming that he or she is back home every night, that person is probably in acceptance and integration.
_____ 7. The cultural adjustment is only psychological; it is not physical.
_____ 8. If students tend to group together and to feel angry (over a long period of time), either with themselves or with the host culture, they are probably in mental isolation.

____ 9. There are generally three high points and two low points in the entry cycle.

____ 10. Only big problems contribute to culture shock.

Vocabulary Words

You can frequently guess the meaning of a word by reading the sentences around it. Find the paragraph in the essay on pages 18–20 with the same number as the number in parentheses. Then find the word that fits the definition and write it in the blank.

Example:

(Paragraph 1) A feeling of being a little angry _____ *(irritability)* _____

(Paragraph 1) A feeling of disappointment and anger _____

(Paragraph 1) A feeling of indignant displeasure _____

(Paragraph 1) A feeling of missing home _____

(Paragraph 1) A feeling of low spirits and sadness _____

(Paragraph 2) To recall, to tell _____

(Paragraph 4) Hints _____

(Paragraph 4) Obscurity or lack of clarity _____

(Paragraph 4) Identify a condition from the symptoms _____

(Paragraph 4) To guide _____

(Paragraph 8) Deep sorrow, sadness because of loss _____

(Paragraph 9) A part one plays _____

(Paragraph 10) To feel contempt or a lack of respect _____

(Paragraph 11) Methods or plans _____

(Paragraph 14) To prove unfaithful _____

Vocabulary Exercise

Complete the blanks with an appropriate vocabulary word from those listed on pages 17 and 22. The answers follow.

1. Many students feel _____ when they first arrive in the United States.

2. A detective uses _____ in order to determine who committed a crime.

3. The friends drove three days _____ from New York to San Francisco. They only stopped to eat three times each day.

4. The little girl felt a lot of _____ when her puppy was killed by a car.

5. I could tell that the little boy was scared and trying to appear brave. He was obviously _____. He was almost crying.

6. My dirty clothes are soaking in soap and water in the kitchen _____.

7. The doctor _____ his illness as asthma.

8. We should volunteer to _____ new students to the campus.

9. It has rained all day but there will be only light _____ tonight.

10. His writing is not clear; it is very _____.

1. homesick 2. cues 3. straight 4. grief 5. fighting back tears 6. sink 7. diagnosed 8. orient 9. showers 10. ambiguous

Word Forms

In English, a noun can be formed from an adjective by adding -ness, -ion, -ity, or -is. Choose the correct word form to fit into the following sentences. Write the part of speech at the end of each sentence (adjective or noun).

Example:
irritability, irritable

1. *The woman was very ___irritable___ when the dog jumped on her. (adj)*

2. *Her ___irritability___ was evident when the dog jumped on her. (noun)*

bitterness, bitter

1. He is _____ about his experience. (   )

2. His _____ about his experience is evident. (   )

homesickness, homesick

1. He is very_____ .(   )

2. His _____ keeps him from studying. (   )

depression, depressed

1. Counselors can help with _____. (   )

2. The boy was very _____ and went to see a counselor. (   )

ambiguity, ambiguous

1. The man answered me in an _____ way. (   )

2. There was a lot of _____ in his answer. (   )

diagnosis, diagnostic

1. The doctor made a good _____ of the disease. (   )

2. The doctor used good _____ tools in his work. (   )

Exercises

Where are you in the process of cultural adaptation? (Hint: If you don't know, ask your classmates where you are.)

In small groups, generate a list of attitudes that would help someone to adjust to a new culture.

In small groups, make a list of things that students can do to facilitate passing through the adjustment process.

THE FOLLOWING BOOKS HAVE MORE INFORMATION
ABOUT CULTURAL ADJUSTMENT:

ADLER, PETER,   "Culture Shock and the Cross-Cultural Learning Experience," in
    Readings in Intercultural Communication, Vol. II, ed. David S. Hoopes. Pitts-
    burgh, PA: Regional Council for International Education of the University of
    Pittsburgh, 1979.
FURNHAM, ADRIAN and STEPHEN BOCHNER,   *Culture Shock*. London, New York:
    Routledge, Chapman and Hall, 1986. **This is a comprehensive study of culture
    shock.**
KIM, YOUNG YUN,   *Communication and Cross-Cultural Adaptation: An Integrative
    Theory*. Multilingual Matters of Clevedon, England, 1988. **This comprehensive
    book includes theory and application about the subject of cultural adaptation
    that are based on ten years' research on Korean, Mexican, Japanese and Indo-
    Chinese immigrants. A very complete book on the subject.**
KOHLS, L. ROBERT,   *Survival Kit for Overseas Living*. Chicago, Illinois: Intercultural
    Press, Inc., 1979. **Although written for Americans who are planning to live in
    other countries, the information is applicable for those who come to live and
    study in the United States also.**
LEWIS, TOM and ROBERT JUNGMAN, eds.,   *On Being Foreign: Culture Shock in Short
    Fiction: An International Anthology*. Yarmouth, Maine: Intercultural Press,
    1986. **This is a collection of twenty short stories that show the adjustment of
    fictional characters in a foreign country.**

SUGGESTIONS FOR LEARNING MORE ABOUT THE PEOPLE'S REPUBLIC
OF CHINA ARE:

Country Studies for the PRC. These are books that have been developed by the Foreign
    Area Studies Group at American University for the Department of Defense and
    other U.S. government agencies. They are available from the Superintendent of
    Documents, U.S. Government Printing Office, Washington, DC 20402.
HSU, FRANCIS L. K.,   *Americans and Chinese: Passages to Differences*. Honolulu, HI:
    University Press of Hawaii, 1953.
KAPP, ROBERT A., ed.,   *Communicating with China*. Chicago: Intercultural Press,
    1983.

Chapter 3

Luz Maria

The story now shifts to the point of view of Luz Maria, a young woman from Colombia who studies with Li Li. As you read about her, notice how she is adapting to her new life in the United States. Is she adapting well or not, in your opinion? What is the significance of her dreams in the story? Do you ever have recurring dreams?

Non-English Words that Appear in the Reading
"Luz Maria Gonzales: Colombia"

sobremesa – the time after a meal when everyone stays at the table talking with one
another

piropo – flirtatious greeting that many men in Latin cultures say to women as they
pass them on the street

LUZ MARIA GONZALES: COLOMBIA

The light shining through the mass of black tangles that **frame** her small face
sparkles in her black eyes. Luz Maria Gonzales left her mother and father, two sisters,
three brothers, and grandmother in Cartagena, Colombia, to come to the university in the
United States. Now after two months, her life back home seems like a dream, except at
night when she dreams of her family and friends and awakes sure that she is in Cartagena.

Her happy dreams disappear as she slowly looks around her dorm room. She lies
in bed, **savoring** the images of her dreams for as long as she can, images of sleeping with
her sister, Katrina, the warmth of their breath mingling as they lay whispering in the
dark. The dream images merge in her mind with memories of her family **lingering**
round the table for the *sobremesas* after dinner, drinking rich, Colombian coffee. Her
heart aches as she mentally views each beloved face around the table.

In Colombia her boyfriend, Jorge, was constantly at her side. They went to class
together, had lunch together, went shopping together, went to parties together—
talking and dancing—always together. She ate at his house and he ate at her house for
three years until they gradually became one. Luz Maria was deeply satisfied in **surren-
dering** every **aspect** of her life to him, trusting him completely. She especially loved
him because he was so tender and gentlemanly with her and her family. She was secure
as his woman.

Here, in the United States, the men seem passionless and untrustworthy. She
even wonders if she has somehow become ugly, missing the constant *piropos* that
accompanied her on the streets of Cartagena (which, of course, she both expected and
ignored) and the daily comments on how pretty she looked from her family and friends.
Back home people showed that they were *really* interested in her. In contrast, her
American roommate, Kathy, only looks at her **intently** on those days when Luz Maria
feels sad. The one time that Luz Maria spoke with her about feeling depressed, Kathy
suggested that she go to the International Student Counseling office on campus,
carefully explaining to her where it was located.

Luz Maria opens her eyes as she hears Kathy move across the room.

"Good morning, Kathy, how did you sleep?"

"Fine, thanks."

"Good, so you are fine this morning?"

"Yeah, I just need some coffee."

The girls move toward the showers.

Luz Maria chatting,

"What will you do today?"

"I dunno, I gotta study; I gotta big calculus exam on Wednesday."

"Oh, maybe I can help you."

The rushing water **drowns** Kathy's reply.

Back in the room, Kathy pulls on a pair of jeans, a red sweater, and boots. The girls stand at the mirror, Luz Maria watching Kathy roll mascara on her lashes. She picks up Kathy's long, blond hair and with a big, red, plastic clip expertly twists it into a roll. Stepping to the side, she says,

"Oh, yes—now you need gold earrings. Here put on these. And some red liptstick."

She rummages in her makeup purse.

"Here. Oh you look beautiful."

Kathy surveys herself in the mirror, raises one eyebrow, and **purses** her lips.

"Yeah, not bad."

She **tilts** her head and smiles broadly.

"Not bad. Thanks Luz. See ya later."

"Good-bye."

Luz Maria snaps on the tape recorder and finishes dressing as the romantic ballads of Roberto Carlos fill the room.

She arrives in class, her gold ankle **bracelet** peeping from beneath the long, full red skirt and gold earring hoops **nestled** in her curls. Leaving her books on the desk, she wanders in the hall, bracelets **jangling** as she puts her hands in her pockets. She leaves an **aromatic** cloud of Chanel No. 5 wherever she moves. She sees her teacher and, checking an impulse to kiss Joy on the cheek, she draws close and says,

"How are you this morning?"

"Fine, Luz Maria, how are you?"

"Fine, thank you."

"Shall we go on in?"

Her day passes (it seems to go much faster here than in Cartagena), **punctuated** by classes, breaks, lunch, and a trip to the post office. After class she, Najwa, Phi, and Li Li go to the campus bookstore where she buys pink **stationery** with a picture of a cute little girl in the corner, a little T-shirt for her nephew, Carlitos, and a larger one for herself, both with the university symbol emblazoned on the front.

After dinner, she returns to her room to do her homework. In the midst of reading the assignment, she suddenly thinks of Jorge. She stops and writes him a letter, **uneasy** at the realization that she had not thought of him all day.

As she drifts off to sleep, she thinks, "I'll ask Kathy tomorrow to go with me to buy some boots like hers." And that night, she dreams for the first time a dream that will **haunt** her for many months. In the dream she is rowing a small boat over calm tropical waters, and she can see Cartagena on the horizon, **looming** larger and larger. Then, an insistent **current** pulls the boat backwards and try as she might, Luz Maria Gonzales cannot get home again.

Vocabulary Words

1. **frame her face**—be around her face
2. **savor**—enjoy very much

3. **linger**—stay; not leave
4. **surrender**—give up or give in to
5. **aspect**—part
6. **look intently**—look with great interest
7. **suggest**—recommend
8. **drown her reply**—not hear her because of the sound of the water
9. **mascara**—brown or black substance for coloring the eyelashes
10. **clip**—an object used to hold something together or in place
11. **twist**—turn around and around
12. **purse lips**—push lips outward
13. **tilt head**—incline the head to one side
14. **bracelet**—jewelry worn around the wrist or ankle
15. **nestled**—placed securely in her hair
16. **jangling**—make a sound like bells
17. **aromatic**—smelling good
18. **punctuated**—broken into pieces
19. **stationery**—the paper used to write letters
20. **uneasy**—troubled
21. **haunt**—persist
22. **loom**—come into sight as through a cloud
23. **current**—a movement of water

Discussion Questions

In small groups, discuss the following questions. Be prepared to share your discussion with the class.

1. Why do you think that Luz Maria felt uneasy when she realized that she had not thought of Jorge all day? Have you had a similar experience about family members, friends, girlfriends, or boyfriends?

2. Why do you think that her day passes faster in the United States than it did in Cartagena? Do you think that time "feels" different here in the United States than it does back in your country? If so, how?

3. What did you learn about Colombian culture from this reading? What kinds of things do you suppose are important for Luz Maria based on the reading? Are these things important in your culture? In American culture?

4. Where is Luz Maria in the cultural adjustment cycle (see page 19)?

TO HOW OR TO WHY:
THAT IS THE QUESTION*

Luz Maria, like all people who live in a foreign culture, needs to get information about that culture. She needs to understand what is happening in her new environment. She, like most people, gets the information in numerous ways. (1)

Learning about Other Cultures

We can learn about a culture by reading books and articles written about that culture. We also learn about other cultures by seeing them portrayed in the media—movies, T.V. programs, or newspaper articles. Still another way to learn is by listening to other people describe their experiences within the other culture and their interpretations of those experiences. (2)

However, most knowledge about a culture is learned at a more subtle level. Luz Maria is learning about Americans at this level. She notices Americans doing or saying something that is different or strange, and either explains it according to her own cultural values or asks someone, usually from her own culture, for an explanation of the behavior. The third possibility (which is done less frequently) is to ask an individual from the other culture. It is learning at this more subtle level that we now analyze in depth. (3)

Noticing Cultural Differences

When we are in a different culture, it is natural to be aware of those things which are different from our own culture, either consciously or unconsciously. For example, when Luz Maria is depressed and talks to Kathy about it, she expects Kathy to listen and discuss her problem. This expectation is based on what friends in Colombia do. She has a "culture bump"† when Kathy suggests that she go to the counseling office. If she were to ask Kathy about this incident, the question might be something like, "Why don't you want to talk to me? Why did you tell me to go there?" No matter the exact question, it would be a "why" question and Kathy might answer as follows: "Because I can't help you. You need a professional." or "Because I want you to feel better." And

---

*"To be or not to be: that is the question." William Shakespeare, *Hamlet.*

†A culture bump occurs when a person has expectations of a particular behavior and gets something different when interacting with individuals from another culture.

given Luz Maria's cultural way of evaluating help, Kathy's answers make no sense. Neither, of course, do Luz Maria's questions make any sense to Kathy. Each of them is talking at the other, unaware of the blinders their cultures have placed on them. (4)

Why Questions

If we analyze the why question, we discover that we are actually asking the person to explain why they are different from us. When Luz Maria noticed a difference in the way that Kathy acted with her, she wondered why. When she asked why, she was actually asking, "Why are you different from my friends in Colombia?" When Kathy answers the question, she is really explaining why she is different from Luz Maria, thus reinforcing the difference between the two cultures. It is possible to ask questions in such a way that we emphasize what we have in common with the other culture rather than reinforcing the differences. (5)

Culture-bound Questions

When we ask questions or answer questions that emphasize the differences, they are culture bound. Culture-bound statements mean that they are rooted in our own unexamined, cultural assumptions. When Luz Maria notices something different from Colombian culture, her noticing, her assumptions, conclusions, questions, and comments are culture bound in Colombian culture. Furthermore, if she interacts with Kathy, Kathy's assumptions, conclusions, and answers are culture bound by American culture. (6)

Culture-free Questions

It is useful to be able to recognize when our questions are culture-bound. With this ability we can then form questions that are less superficial and are more comprehensive. They allow us to have a deeper level of understanding of ourselves and of others. In addition, the culture-free question frequently elicits a more thoughtful response. (7)

How Questions

So, if Luz Maria were to analyze the situation, she would discover that it is actually a universal one: how friends help friends who have a problem. In Colombia, friends frequently tell one another all their problems and give one another advice. These behaviors are considered to be the behaviors of good friends. She would also realize that she doesn't know exactly how Americans judge whether people are good friends. However, she can now ask a different question of Kathy (or any other American) and receive valuable information that is accurate. The question now becomes, "How do Americans express close friendships?" Since friendship exists in all cultures, this more generic question is culture free. (8)

In the first instance we are unaware of our cultural blindness. And trying to answer a culture-bound question is like trying to explain colors to a blind person. However, once she becomes aware of her cultural blindness, Luz Maria can garner useful information about the other culture—information about how Americans see themselves—rather than asking them to explain how she sees them. And in order to accurately judge Americans, one must use their cultural standards. (9)

Comprehension Questions

Put an F by those statements that are false and a T by those that are true. Rewrite the false statements so that they are true.

_____ 1. We can get information about a culture only by reading books.
_____ 2. We usually ask people from the other culture when we don't understand something about that culture.
_____ 3. Luz Maria expects Kathy to react to her as her friends in Colombia do.
_____ 4. When we ask a why question, we are actually asking the other person to explain why they are the same as we are.
_____ 5. Why questions actually reinforce the differences between two cultures.
_____ 6. Why questions are culture free.
_____ 7. How questions are usually culture free.
_____ 8. Culture-bound questions get answers that are also culture bound.
_____ 9. How questions ask about universal situations rather than cultural characteristics.
_____ 10. Our own cultural standards are always sufficient to understand another culture.

Vocabulary Words

You can frequently guess the meaning of a word by reading the sentences around it. Find the paragraph in the essay on pages 31–33 with the same number as the number in parentheses. Then find the word that fits the definition and write it in the blank.

Example:

(Paragraph 3) Delicate, hardly noticeable _____ subtle _____

(Paragraph 3) Profound, deep, thorough _____

(Paragraph 4) What you think will happen _____

(Paragraph 4) To judge, give an opinion _____

(Paragraph 4) Limit on one's vision or understanding _____

(Paragraph 5) To strengthen, encourage, reassure _____

(Paragraph 5) To give importance to, to stress _____

(Paragraph 6) Ethnocentric _____

(Paragraph 6) To talk with _____

(Paragraph 7) Shallow, not in depth _____

(Paragraph 7) Complete _____

(Paragraph 7) To bring out, to draw out _____

(Paragraph 8) Precise, exactly _____

(Paragraph 8) General, not specific _____

(Paragraph 8) Not ethnocentric _____

(Paragraph 9) To gather, to collect _____

Vocabulary Exercise

Fill in the blanks with vocabulary words listed on pages 29 and 30. The answers follow.

1. The teacher _____ that he read extra material outside of class.

2. I feel _____ about my sister not calling today. I'm afraid she had an accident.

3. The party was so great that we wanted to _____ after the other guests had left.

4. The doctor needs to _____ the tests to see if the patient is o.k. now.

5. The young girl doesn't use makeup—only a little _____ on her eyelashes.

6. The boat floated down the river, following the rushing _____.

7. The essay was too short and didn't go into enough detail. It was very _____.

8. The soldiers had to _____ to the enemy because they didn't have any ammunition.

9. The kid walked down the street with his hands in his pockets _____ his money.

10. The actor had won many prizes; he had spent many years _____ honors.

1. suggested 2. uneasy 3. linger 4. evaluate 5. mascara 6. current 7. superficial 8. surrender 9. jangling 10. garnering

Word Forms

In English, an adverb can be formed by adding an -ly to an adjective. Choose the correct word form to fit into each sentence. Write the part of speech at the end of each sentence (adjective or adverb).

Example:
subtle, subtly

1. She was very _____subtle_____ in her suggestion to me. (adj)

2. She suggested _____subtly_____ that I do this. (adv)

unexpected, unexpectedly

1. The teacher's visit was totally _____. (   )

2. My friend came to my house last night _____. (   )

superficial, superficially

1. His anger was only _____. (   )

2. He was only _____ angry. (   )

comprehensive, comprehensively

1. Her knowledge of geography is _____. (   )

2. She studied geography _____. (   )

accurate, accurately

1. He answered the question _____. (   )

2. He gave an _____ answer to the question. (   )

generic, generically

1. She uses a _____ brand of medicine. (   )

2. Rather than answering the question specifically, she answered it _____.
   (   )

Culture-bound and Culture-free Practice

Place a CB by those statements that are culture bound and a CF by those that are culture free. Check your answers with a classmate.

____ 1. Why do the women wear veils?
____ 2. How do they feel about wearing veils?
____ 3. Why don't the grandparents live with the family?
____ 4. How come they drive so fast?
____ 5. Why are the teachers so friendly?
____ 6. How do they know if a teacher is good or not?

Practice analyzing how and why questions. Notice that why questions follow this pattern: (1) Why do they do what they do? (2) Why don't they do what we do? (3) Why are they different from us? How questions follow this pattern: (1) How do they do what we do? (2) How are they the same as us?

Complete each sentence as in the first example. Notice that each question emphasizes either a difference between cultures or a similarity between cultures. Discuss your answers with a partner.

Example: Why do you go to work so early?
          a. Why do you not go to work at the same time that I do?
          b. Why are you different from me?

1. Why do American children leave home when they are 18?
   a. Why...
   b. Why...
2. Why do American old people live alone?
   a. Why...
   b. Why
3. How do Americans show respect for their old people?
   a. How...

Which questions make you feel closer and more comfortable with American people?
Why?
What is the difference in the kind of information that each type of question elicits?
What are the advantages and disadvantages of each type of question?

Worksheet on Cultural Questioning

Recall an experience that you have had with a person from another culture. Did they do
or say anything that was different for you? Yes   No

If yes, what was it?

Do you think you understand why they did it? Yes   No

If yes, did you explain the behavior to yourself or did you ask someone about it?

If you asked someone, whom did you ask?

List possible questions that you might ask an individual from the other culture about
that behavior.

1.

2.

3.

4.

5.

Put a CB by those questions that you feel are culture bound.
Put a CF by those that you feel are culture free.
Check your answers with a classmate.
If someone from that culture is in your class, ask him or her the questions. Notice
whether his or her answers are culture bound or culture free.

Crossword Vocabulary Review

Using the vocabulary words listed on pages 5, 9, 18, 22, 29, 30, and 34, fill in blanks in the puzzle.

ACROSS
1. short name
5. feeling of indignant displeasure
8. jewelry worn around the wrist or ankle
11. to encourage, to create
12. echo
13. precise, exactly
14. job, work
15. smelling good
17. to influence
18. to guide
20. hints
21. to come into sight as though through a cloud
22. paper used to write letters

DOWN
2. to recall, to tell
3. placed securely
4. series of pictures
6. brown or black substance for coloring eyelashes
7. to gather, to collect
9. to bring out, to draw out
10. big, huge
11. Not the truth
12. to keep
16. a movement of water
19. feeling of missing home (adjective)

Answers on page 40.

FOR MORE INFORMATION ON CULTURE-BOUND AND CULTURE-FREE ATTITUDES:

HALL, EDWARD T., *Beyond Culture*. Garden City, NY: Anchor Press/Doubleday, 1976. **A classic explanation of the influence of culture on an individual.**
WURZEL, JAIME S., *Toward Multiculturism: A Reader in Multicultural Education*. Yarmouth, Maine: Intercultural Press, Inc., 1988.

FOR MORE INFORMATION ABOUT COLOMBIA:

GIL, FEDERICO, *Latin American–United States Relations*. New York/Chicago/San Francisco/Atlanta: Harcourt Brace Jovanovich, Inc., 1971. **Provides a comprehensive analysis of the historical relationship between the United States and the various Latin American countries.**
GORDON, RAYMOND L., *Living in Latin America: A Case Study in Cross-Cultural Communication*. Lincolnwood, IL: National Textbook, 1974. **A book based on interviews with Americans who lived with Colombians and the Colombians with whom they lived. Deals with the differences in how Colombians and Americans view home.**
MARQUEZ, GABRIEL GARCIA, trans. GREGORY RABASSA, *One Hundred Years of Solitude*. New York: Harper and Row, 1970. **A masterpiece by a Nobel Prize winner.**

Answer to puzzle on page 38

Chapter 4

Abdul Aziz

In this story, Abdul Aziz, the undergraduate student from Saudi Arabia who studies with Luz and Li Li, invites their American classmate, Brian, to his apartment to study together. As you read the story, notice the things that are important to Aziz. Do you think they would be important for most Saudis? Notice also what Aziz expects Brian to do and then what happens when Brian doesn't do what he expects.

Non-English Words that Appear in the Reading
"Abdul Aziz: Saudi Arabia"

thobes – long, white robes worn by males in Saudi Arabia

Bedouin – nomadic tribes in Saudi Arabia

heil – (cardamom) a spice used in coffee in Saudi Arabia

capsa – a Saudi dish with chicken or lamb and rice

hummus – ground chick peas

tabouli – an Arabic salad

Allah – God

Kaaba – a holy place for Muslims in the city of Mecca

bakhoor – a wood that gives a sweet smell when burned

mubkhara – a container in which bakhoor is burned

Ahlan wa sahlan – Welcome

Tafaddla – Come in; sit down

abaya – a long, black cloth that women in Saudi Arabia use to cover themselves when they are outside the home

ABDUL AZIZ AL-AHMED: SAUDI ARABIA

Even in western clothes, his movements reflect the dignity of his father and his father's father as they strode the deserts of Saudi Arabia, their white *thobes* whipping **in the fierce desert wind.** His Arabic language had been fed by centuries of *Bedouin* poetry that celebrated the flight of **falcons,** of shifting **desert dunes,** and of awesome nighttime skies that dwarf lowly man. And now as he moves through the university's hallways, crowded with **flaxen-haired** youth, his dark eyes lowered before blue jean clad girls, his thoughts turn to his home in Riyadh.

Riyadh and the white stone villa, surrounded by a high stone fence where he'd lived all his life with his father, mother, his father's mother, three brothers, two sisters-in-law, a sister, and four nephews. In his imagination, he pushed open the heavy metal gates, fronting on the **barren** street, and felt the blue and yellow tiled path beneath his feet. His **nostrils** widened with hot air heavy with jasmine. In the house, he heard the murmur of voices from the women's living room. He passed in to the interior courtyard where Nabil and Karim (aged four and five) ran around the tiled fountain. A smile crossed his face as he mentally **scolded** them for throwing a large pink, plastic fish into the water. Then a **sting of loneliness** clasped his heart and misted over his eyes. A deep breath locked the pain in his heart, only to escape at those odd moments that a sight, a sound, or a smell **dissolved the protective shield** of his heart.

As he settled into his seat, he noticed Brian sitting in the front row. A knot of anger rose in his throat as Saturday's humiliation flooded back. His hand trembled slightly taking out his notebook as he recalled his foolish excitement at having an American friend.

Back home, his intense friendship with his cousin Najeeb and Abdulla was total, woven into the **fabric** of his daily life, and it felt as though his very soul had been **ripped apart** when he left. So when Brian had suggested coming by his apartment to study together, he had been filled with anticipation.

He had rushed to the Middle Eastern Specialty Shop after class on Friday to buy dates, cardamom for the coffee, and a fresh chicken. Early Saturday morning, he had awakened and begun to prepare *capsa,* recalling his mother's instructions, chopped parsley and tomatoes to mix with lemon juice for *tabouli* and ground up garbanzos to make *hummus.* He rushed back to buy Arabic bread fresh from the oven and to pick up two cartons of Pepsi. And then, remembering Americans' eating habits, he went back and bought potato chips and dip.

When Brian entered the **sparse** apartment, he was greeted by the smell of rice and chicken and *bakhoor* burning in an ornate silver *mubkhara.* He immediately noticed a gold **plaque** of the word *Allah* hanging beside a prayer rug with the *Kaaba* on it. Aziz welcomed his guest and offered him pungent, light-green coffee in a small cup. The bitter taste drew tears to Brian's eyes as he said,

"Interesting taste. Got any chips?"

"Of course."

Aziz smiled inwardly at his cleverness in anticipating his guest's needs.

"Listen, can I use your phone a minute?"

"Of course, it is not necessary to ask."

While Brian was **chatting** with a friend, Ziad and Nabil came to the door.

"*Ahlan wa sahlan.* "

"*Tafaddla.* "

Aziz was acutely aware of Brian's continuing to speak, seemingly ignoring the newcomers. His discomfort grew as he poured a second round of coffee and Brian continued his conversation without greeting Ziad and Nabil. He felt the embarrassment of his friends for him when Brian finally hung up, and then with a grin said,

"Hi, my name's Brian. Are you guys from Arabia too?"

Then after a few minutes in which Ziad, Nabil, and he were just beginning to get relaxed and to talk with Brian, Brian announced,

"Well listen, it looks like you're gonna be busy with dinner and your friends. I think I'll just go on over to the library to study."

Despite Aziz's repeated invitations to have one more coffee and to eat, Brian left.

And now looking at the back of Brian's blond head, Aziz resolved to endure the next four years until he could return to the warmth and certainty that was home.

Vocabulary Words

1. **whipping in the fierce desert wind**—blowing in the strong desert wind
2. **falcon**—a bird trained for hunting
3. **desert dunes**—hills of sand in the desert

4. **flaxen haired**—blonde haired
5. **barren**—nothing growing there
6. **nostrils**—the external opening of the nose
7. **to scold**—to rebuke
8. **sting of loneliness**—sharp feeling of loneliness
9. **dissolved the protective shield**—destroyed the protective cover
10. **fabric**—material
11. **ripped apart**—torn into pieces
12. **sparse**—without much furniture
13. **plaque**—a flat, metal ornament hung on the wall
14. **to chat**—to speak informally about unimportant things

Discussion Questions

In small groups, discuss the following questions. Be prepared to share your discussion with the class.

1. What do you suppose will happen the next time that an American invites Aziz to do something?

2. Do you think that Brian knew that Aziz was upset? Have you had a similar experience?

3. Where is Aziz in the cultural adjustment cycle? (See page 19.) Give specific examples to explain your answer. (*Note:* He may be in more than one stage.)

SOWING CULTURE BUMPS

While living in another culture, we find some things that are the same as in our own country. In these instances, the two cultures fit together. However, there are other things that are different. The points at which the two cultures differ or "bump into each other" are usually the areas that interfere in the development of successful cross-cultural relationships. If the specific points of difference, or culture bumps, are analyzed, they can lead to a deeper understanding. If they are not analyzed, they can lead to stereotypes of people in the other culture. (1)

The Source of Stereotypes

Aziz has just formed stereotypes of Americans that are commonly held by many Arabs as well as other internationals. Some of these stereotypes are that Americans are "cold," "unfriendly," or "mechanical." We can understand how this has happened by examining the "seed" from which the stereotype grew. That "seed" is called a culture bump. (2)

Definition of a Culture Bump

A culture bump occurs when an individual has expectations of a particular behavior within a particular situation and receives a different behavior when interacting with individuals from another culture. Expectations as used in the definition refer to the expectations of "normal" behavior as learned in one's own culture. Aziz expects women in Saudi Arabia in public places to be accompanied by males and to wear a black *abaya* and a black face veil. He, of course, knew even before he left Saudi Arabia that women in the United States would act and dress differently. Yet he has a culture bump when he sees "blue jean clad girls" in the university's hallways, simply because it is different than it would be in Saudi Arabia. (3)

While he expected American women to dress and behave differently from Saudi women, he didn't expect Brian to continue to talk on the phone as other visitors arrived. He expected Brian to stop talking, to greet the guests, and then to continue his conversation. This culture bump was a surprise. And he certainly was unaware of the following culture bump, namely Brian's (seemingly) hasty exit; he expected Brian to stay and talk, drink and eat for several hours, and then to have dinner together. His culture had taught him that to not eat and "be" with friends was an insult, or perhaps a way of saying, "I'm angry with you." (4)

Characteristics of Culture Bumps

Culture bumps are positive, negative, or neutral. They are positive if the one having them likes the behavior; they are negative if one doesn't like them (e.g., Aziz felt humiliated when Brian didn't greet his guests or eat his food). And they are neutral if one doesn't care or has become accustomed to the behavior (e.g., after several months in the United States, Aziz is accustomed to unaccompanied, unveiled females in public). Since it depends on the individual, the idea about a culture bump can change. For example, Aziz might have felt uncomfortable the first couple of times that he saw an unaccompanied, unveiled American woman in public. However, he is now accustomed to this sight and the same culture bump is now neutral. (5)

Culture bumps occur continuously when we are with anyone from another culture. Therefore, while Aziz is having culture bumps with Brian, Brian is also having them with Aziz. And neither of them is aware of the consequences of these seemingly minor incidents. Neither takes advantage of his culture bumps in order to more deeply understand himself and the other. (6)

Comprehension Questions

Put an F by those statements that are false and a T by those that are true. Rewrite the false statements so that they are true.

_____ 1. It is impossible to find any areas of commonality between two cultures.

_____ 2. Unexamined culture bumps can lead to stereotypes of the other people.

_____ 3. If someone knows that people in the other culture will act differently, then he or she will not have culture bumps.

_____ 4. If someone becomes accustomed to the different behavior, he or she no longer has a culture bump.

_____ 5. Culture bumps are always bad.

_____ 6. If a culture bump is negative, it will always be negative.

_____ 7. Culture bumps happen frequently when we are with someone from another culture.

_____ 8. We can only have a culture bump if we are in a foreign country.

_____ 9. Culture bumps can be very useful.

_____ 10. Culture bumps do not usually interfere with cross-cultural relationships.

Vocabulary Words

You can frequently guess the meaning of a word by reading the sentences around it. Find the paragraph in the essay on pages 44–46 with the same number as the number in parentheses. Then find the word that fits the definition and write it in the blank.

Example:

(Paragraph 1) To plant _____ *to sow* _____

(Paragraph 1) Cultural differences _____

(Paragraph 2) Opinion about a group of people _____

(Paragraph 3) Only _____

(Paragraph 4) Quick _____

(Paragraph 5) Good _____

(Paragraph 5) Bad _____

(Paragraph 5) Neither good nor bad _____

(Paragraph 5) Extremely embarrassed _____

Vocabulary Exercise

Fill in the blanks with vocabulary words listed on pages 43, 44, 46, and 47. The answers follow.

1. I went to town and bought some _____ to make a new dress.

2. He blew his nose so much that his _____ were all red and tender.

3. The desert appears to be very _____ with nothing growing there.

4. The neighbors meet in their yards in the evenings and _____ for about an hour.

5. The farmer _____ his seeds every springtime.

6. I was so embarrassed and _____ when the teacher yelled at me in class.

7. The school gave the principal a _____ honoring him for his years of service.

8. The _____ flew over our heads, crying in the wind.

9. The mother _____ her little boy when he spilled his milk on the table.

10. Newly arrived students from other countries sometimes form opinions or _____

    _____ about Americans that are inaccurate.

1. material 2. nostrils 3. barren or sparse 4. chat 5. sows 6. humiliated 7. plaque 8. falcons 9. scolded 10. stereotypes

Word Forms

In this exercise, practice forming adverbs from adjectives. Remember: to form an adverb, add an -ly to the end of an adjective. Write the part of speech at the end of each sentence (v., adj., adv., n.).

Example:

simply, simple

   1. He had a _____simple_____ idea. (adj.)

   2. She is _____simply_____ a child. (adv.)

hasty, hastily

   1. We went _____ to the house. (   )

   2. We were _____ as we went to the house. (   )

positive, positively

   1. She reacted _____ when I told her the news. (   )

   2. She was _____ about the news that I told her. (   )

negative, negatively

   1. They had a _____ reaction to the book. (   )

   2. They acted _____ as they read the book. (   )

neutral, neutrally

   1. Switzerland was _____ during World War II. (   )

   2. Switzerland acted _____ during World War II. (   )

Culture-Bump Worksheet

Write a definition of a culture bump in your own words.

A culture bump is:

_____

_____

Form groups of individuals from similar cultures. Together make a list of at least three culture bumps that you all agree upon. A culture bump is a specific incident. To make sure that you are listing incidents, check them to make sure that they tell who, what, where, and when. For example:

I saw an American go into a grocery store with no shoes on.

Who was it ? (An American)
What did they do? (They went barefoot into a store)
Where did they do it? (A grocery store)
When did they do it? (The first week I arrived in the United States)

1.

Who _____

What _____

Where _____

When _____

2.

Who _____

What _____

Where _____

When _____

3.

Who _____

What _____

Where _____

When _____

THE FOLLOWING BOOKS HAVE MORE INFORMATION ABOUT CULTURE BUMPS:

ARCHER, CAROL M., "Beyond Culture Bumps," in *Culture Bound*, ed. Joyce M. Valdes. Cambridge, England, and New York: Cambridge University Press, 1986.
BARNAK, PAULA, HENRY HOLMES, and STEPHEN GUILD, *Intercultural Sourcebook*, eds. David S. Hoopes and Paul Ventura. LaGrange Park, IL: Intercultural Network, 1979, pp. 132–40.

THE FOLLOWING HAVE MORE INFORMATION ABOUT SAUDI ARABIA:

ALLEN, ROGER, *Modern Arabic Literature*. New York: Ungar Pub., 1987.
NAWWAB, ISMAIL I., PETER C. SPEERS, and PAUL F. HOYE, eds., *Aramco and Its World: Arabia and the Middle East*. Dahahra, Saudi Arabia: Aramco, 1980.
YUSUF, ABDULLAH ALI, *The Holy Qur-an: Text, Translation and Commentary*. 2 Vols. New York: Lahore, 1934.
PBS series: "The Saudis"; "Saudi Arabia: Oasis of the Sea."

Chapter 5

Brian Nelson

Brian's visit to Abdul's apartment is told again, but this time from Brian's point of view. As you read the story, notice how Brian's expectations and perceptions differ from Abdul's. How does this story reflect the ideas about perception that were discussed in Chapter 1?

BRIAN NELSON:
UNITED STATES OF AMERICA

It was, perhaps, **stirrings** of a lost boyhood friendship that prompted Brian to suggest to the dark-eyed Arab in his class that they study together on the following Saturday. For that summer when Brian Nelson was 10 years old, his best friend, a Mexican boy next door named Juan Carlos, moved with his family to Chicago. Brian, **long limbed, freckled** with **sandy** hair, deeply missed the **dusky-skinned,** brown-eyed Juan Carlos. That was also the summer that his Mom and Dad got **divorced.** And oh how he missed his Dad those hot August days.

But Brian and his sister, Tammy, had **little time to spare** now. With their Dad gone and their Mom working as a secretary, they **scrounged** their working-class neighborhood for part-time jobs. These jobs plus their increased **chores** at home made them grow up fast. They developed that independent wisdom that is peculiar to **latchkey** kids. They were full partners with their Mom in the struggle **to make a living.**

By the time that he reached his senior year in high school, Brian had made applications to 15 universities, had applied for several student loans, and had saved $2,300 for his first year at school. He and his Mom knew it would be a struggle to get the tuition and dorm fees each year. Now in his last year at the university, Brian reflected on his luck in working as a **surveyor** each summer. Carrying 15 credit hours and working 25 hours at the Burger King left him little time for studying. His easy **drawl** and open smile **belied** a young man in a hurry—in a hurry to pay back his student loans, to graduate, to get to work, to buy his mom a new car—a young man in a hurry to get somewhere in life.

Brian had always been interested in other countries and that fascination had been **nurtured** by his encounters with classmates in the Ft. Worth public schools from Vietnam and Central America. Brian felt that their neighborhood was **pallid** in comparison to those exotic places. So he particularly enjoyed his cross-cultural communication class where he could have personal interactions with students from all over the world. He also hoped that this personal experience would help him to understand the cultural **dimension** of international business. Even in high school, he had eagerly taken extra courses in international studies including a class about the Middle East. In fact, as he drove to Abdul Aziz's apartment he was thinking of that class and of an article about Saudi Arabia in **National Geographic Magazine** that had photographs of kings, camel races, and men with beards and long white dresses. Brian had looked forward to studying with Abdul Aziz, even though he normally studied better and faster alone. This Saturday was a luxury he was allowing himself, to know more about this Saudi from a land so strange.

But when he arrived at the expensive apartment with its strange smells, he felt shy and out of place. He felt embarrassed and inferior as he imagined Abdul Aziz walking into Mom's living room with the blue velvet sofa still covered with plastic and the garage that had been converted into a **den.** Then he immediately felt ashamed and disloyal for feeling embarrassed.

His discomfort grew when Abdul Aziz gave him a small china cup with light green coffee and began to ask about his mother, his family, and his health. He began to feel very awkward and, to cover up his discomfort, asked to use the phone to call his friend, Tom.

While talking on the phone, he noticed the other two Saudis come in and admired their grace as they sat on the floor, drinking coffee. He felt more and more like an **unsophisticated jerk.** He listened to them speaking Arabic in the background and wondered if they were talking about him. The phone line seemed his only **link** to something familiar. But, at last, he forced himself to hang up.

Sitting awkwardly on the floor with the three men, his **mind raced** trying to find things to talk about. And finally, he grabbed at an excuse to leave, then became more uncomfortable as Abdul Aziz insisted that he stay. He felt like he couldn't stay and he couldn't leave either. Finally, after what seemed like an hour, he left—disappointed in himself. Once outside he felt somehow reassured at the normality of life, of 7-11 stores, cars, and billboards, and yet, disappointed that real life wasn't like National Geographic pictures. As he drove down the freeway, a **nagging** doubt deep inside whispered that he had missed an opportunity.

Vocabulary Words

1. **stirrings**—memories
2. **long limbed**—long arms and legs
3. **freckled**—small brown dots on the face
4. **sandy hair**—blonde hair
5. **dusky skinned**—dark skinned
6. **divorced**—ended a marriage legally
7. **little time to spare**—little extra time
8. **scrounge**—search everywhere
9. **chores**—jobs at home
10. **latchkey kids**—children who stay by themselves because their parents are working
11. **make a living**—earn money to live
12. **surveyor**—one who measures land
13. **drawl**—speak slowly
14. **belied**—covered up
15. **nurture**—help to grow
16. **pallid**—not interesting
17. **National Geographic Magazine**—magazine with articles and photos about different countries
18. **den**—the room in a house where the family watches TV and relaxes
19. **unsophisticated**—not clever in the ways of the world
20. **link**—connection
21. **mind raced**—thought quickly
22. **nagging doubt**—insistent doubt
23. **dimension**—aspect, part

Discussion Questions

In small groups, discuss the following questions. Be prepared to share your discussion with the class.

1. Based on the reading, what did you learn about American culture? What are some things that are important for Americans? Are they important in your culture?

2. Why was Brian ashamed of being embarrassed? Have you had a similar experience?

3. What is the opportunity that Brian missed?

REAPING STEREOTYPES

Brian's culture bumps include the room decorations—plaques with Allah written on them, prayer rugs on the wall, and incense burning—none of which even vaguely resemble the rock posters he would expect to find on the living room walls of a university classmate. Nor would he expect a male classmate to cook a meal or to greet him by standing, shaking his hand, and asking about his family. Arabic language is also a culture bump simply because it is different from what he normally hears—English. Brian is aware that Saudis are "different" but living daily with the differences is quite distinct from reading about "them." Both Brian and Aziz expected to study and to get to know one another. However, their expectations differed in that Aziz expected to visit with Brian first and then to study, while Brian expected to study and to visit with Aziz afterwards. (1)

Personalizing Culture Bumps

When we analyze how people normally handle a culture bump, we see that it is usually pigeon holed as something they do or as unusual behavior on the part of that particular individual. The incident is perceived as personal. Either "they" *(the people in that culture)* bother me or he or she bothers me. We can talk about it only in personal terms. "Those Arabs bother me or he, as an individual, bothers me." (2)

Depersonalizing Culture Bumps

But when we say, "I have a culture bump," two things happen. First, it **depersonalizes** the incident and places it in the context of a cultural conflict so it is less of a personal affront to oneself. Second, it returns control of the situation to oneself rather than having them, or he or she, doing it to me. They are simply "being" cultural and we are reacting. The way in which we verbalize our experiences is important in how we feel about those experiences. (3)

Mirroring

But whether it is disposed of as cultural or as individual behavior, it is examined from the point of view that "they/he/she" are different rather than "I/we" are different. If we discuss the incident, we almost always do so with individuals from our own culture. Rarely do we check out our culture bumps with people from the other culture. Thus, we can easily picture Abdul Aziz, Ziad, and Nabil sitting in the living room after Brian leaves, having the following conversation. (4)

Ziad: Don't worry my friend. I have been here 7 years. Americans are like this—always in a hurry.

Nabil: Yes, Americans are interested only in money and to work. That is why I am returning home each summer, to have the feeling of community.

Aziz: Yes, here my neighbors do not care for me. This morning I said good morning to my neighbor. He only smiled and said good morning. He did not speak with me or ask anything about me. How can we trust one another if we can't speak together as friends and neighbors to know one another?

Ziad: Yes, they are like that. (5)

And, of course, we can also hear Brian's conversation with his American friend, Tom, at the library.

Brian: You know that Arab guy in my communication class?

Tom: Yeah, why?

Brian: I wuz gonna to study with him today, but he had all these other guys over there, sitting around on the floor, talking. I dunno, I felt weird.

Tom: Yeah, I knew some guys from over there somewhere. They're always sticking together. Nice, but I remember going over to their place. It was the same thing. Man, they had tons of food and it was nice but too much—ya know? Somehow I just don't trust them.

Brian: Yeah, I know what you mean. (6)

Both Brian and Aziz have checked out their assumptions with people they trust, people from their own background, but unwittingly, have merely looked at their own reflection in a mirror. This process, not surprisingly, is called mirroring. And, as a result, both now are confirmed in their impressions of the other. Thus are the seeds of a stereotype sown. Ultimately, to unravel the stereotype, we must recognize, define, and properly name our experiences with people different from ourselves. (7)

Comprehension Questions

Put an F by those statements that are false and a T by those that are true. Rewrite the false statements so that they are true.

_____ 1. Brian had very few culture bumps because he already had read a lot about Saudi Arabia and knew they were quite different from Americans.

_____ 2. Because language is not culture, hearing Arabic spoken was not a culture bump for Brian.

_____ 3. When people have a culture bump, they usually think it is something strange or different that people from the other culture do.

_____ 4. The words that we use to describe our experiences with people from other cultures are not important.

_____ 5. When someone says, "I had a culture bump," he or she is depersonalizing the incident.

_____ 6. When we have a culture bump, we usually ask people from the other culture for an explanation of what happened.

_____ 7. Americans are interested only in money and in working.

_____ 8. Arabs cannot be trusted; they are false friends.

_____ 9. Checking your assumptions about people from another culture with people from your own culture is called mirroring.

_____ 10. Mirroring is the best way to understand other cultures.

Vocabulary Words

You can frequently guess the meaning of a word by reading the sentences around it. Find the paragraph in the essay on pages 54–56 with the same number as the number in the parentheses. Then find the word that fits the definition and write it in the blank.

Example:

(Paragraph 1) Natural substance that smells nice when burned _____ *incense* _____

(Paragraph 1) Not clearly _____

(Paragraph 2) Deal with, manage _____

(Paragraph 2) Classify, categorize _____

(Paragraph 3) Insult _____

(Paragraph 3) Make objective _____

(Paragraph 3) To respond to something _____

(Paragraph 4) Get rid of, finish with _____

(Paragraph 6) Strange _____

(Paragraph 6) Stay together _____

(Paragraph 7) Unintentionally _____

(Paragraph 7) Image _____

(Paragraph 7) To see yourself _____

(Paragraph 7) Make sure, give proof _____

(Paragraph 7) Undo _____

Vocabulary Exercise

Fill in the blanks with vocabulary words listed on pages 53, 56, and 57. The answers follow.

1. The husband and wife fought so much that they finally got a _____.

2. I can't remember that night very well. I _____ recall some things from that night.

3. I saw my _____ in the store window and was surprised at how I looked.

4. I called the airlines and _____ my reservation to New York.

5. People from the South frequently speak with a _____.

6. Staying out in the sun will sometimes cause _____ on my face.

7. In the Catholic Church, the priest burns _____ at certain times in the ceremony.

8. I had to _____ for enough money to pay the bills this month.

9. I have been so sick that I look very _____. But once I get out into the sun, I will return to my normal color.

10. It is very expensive for the city to _____ of all the garbage.

1. divorce 2. vaguely 3. reflection 4. confirmed 5. drawl 6. freckles 7. incense 8. scrounge 9. pallid 10. dispose

Word Forms

In English, the past participle of a verb can be used as an adjective. In this exercise, choose the correct word form to fit into the following sentences. Write the part of speech at the end of each sentence (verb or adjective).

Example:
to pigeon hole, pigeon holed

1. *I _____pigeon holed_____ his behavior as abnormal. (verb)*

2. *His behavior was _____pigeon holed_____ as abnormal. (adjective)*

to depersonalize, depersonalized

1. The course helped us _____ our experience. (   )

2. After the course, our experience had been _____. (   )

to stick together, stuck together

1. Those students are always _____. (   )

2. Those students always _____. ('   )

to reflect, reflected

1. The mirror _____ her image. (   )

2. Her image was _____ in the mirror. (   )

to confirm, confirmed

1. She _____ her reservations. (   )

2. Her reservations are _____. (   )

to unravel, unraveled

1. The sweater is _____. (   )

2. The cat _____ the sweater. (   )

Exercises

In small groups, answer the following questions. The first one is completed as an example.

Carlos (Argentina) and Joe (USA) had an appointment at 3:00. Joe arrived at 3:00. Carlos arrived at 3:20.

Write three ways that Joe might express what happened.

1. As a personal incident. *Carlos must have had a problem* or *Carlos is rude.*
2. As a judgment about Latins. *Latins are always late* or *Latins have a different sense of time than we do.*
3. As a cultural difference. *I had a culture bump with Carlos.*

Wu Jang (PRC) passes a stranger (USA) on the street. The stranger smiles and nods his head.

Write three ways that Wu Jang might express what happened.

1. As a personal incident.
2. As a judgment about Americans.
3. As a cultural difference.

Mehran (Iran) is visiting Frank (USA), for the first time, at Frank's apartment. They are classmates. Frank says, "Come in, I'm on the phone. Make yourself at home. There's beer and soda in the refrigerator."

Write three ways that Mehran might express what happened.

1. As a personal incident.
2. As a judgment about Americans.
3. As a cultural difference.

REVIEW QUESTIONS CHAPTERS 1–5

1. The study of how to live with and communicate with people who are culturally different from oneself is called:
   a. cross-cultural communication
   b. intercultural communication
   c. both a and b
2. Cultural values include:
   a. beliefs, religion, and ideas
   b. beliefs and religion
   c. beliefs
3. Americans are a friendly people. This is:
   a. a descriptive observation
   b. a judgmental observation
   c. both a and b
4. He was sad. This is:
   a. a descriptive observation
   b. a judgmental observation
   c. both a and b
5. Many American children have specific chores to do at home. This is:
   a. a descriptive observation
   b. a judgmental observation
   c. both a and b
6. Carlos and Ming took the same test. Afterwards, Carlos said, "Wow, that test was too hard. It was unfair." Ming replied, "What do you mean? It was easy." This is an example of:
   a. a good student and a bad student talking
   b. the teacher likes Ming better than Carlos
   c. a difference in perceptions
7. Why do Americans call before coming to visit friends? This question is an example of:
   a. a culture-bound question
   b. a culture-free question
   c. neither a nor b
8. How come the Japanese bow when they greet one another? This question is an example of:
   a. a culture-bound question
   b. a culture-free question
   c. neither a nor b
9. How do Colombians express responsibility? This question is an example of:
   a. a culture-bound question
   b. a culture-free question
   c. neither a nor b
10. Mary: You know those Chinese students always make the best grades.
    Sue: Yeah, they always beat everybody else.

This is an example of two American students who are:
a. mirroring
b. having a culture bump
c. neither a nor b

Answer the following questions using complete sentences.

1. Define ethnocentrism. Discuss what happens when foreign students in the United States are ethnocentric, when their American classmates are ethnocentric, and when their teachers are ethnocentric.
2. Explain the difference between a why question and a how question. Discuss the advantages and disadvantages of each type of question.
3. In the following scene, identify at least four culture bumps from the point of view of any of the characters.

   Characters: Mary Jones (North American female)
   Yin Lee (Chinese male)
   Maria Gomez (Puerto Rican female)
   Abdou Al-Khouri (Iraqi male)
   Chihomi Masamoto (Japanese female)
   Mourad Bensouila (Algerian male)

   Abdou is sitting at a table in the cafeteria, drinking coffee. His friend, Yin Lee, comes up and says, "May I sit down?" "Of course," and Abdou motions to a chair. Mourad and Chihomi join them also. Mary Jones arrives with her cup of coffee. Maria Gomez arrives, saying "Hello" and kisses each person on the cheek. She sits next to Mourad and Chihomi and begins to talk, "Oh Chihomi, your hair is beautiful—I love it." She touches Chihomi's hair admiringly. Abdou, sitting beside Mary and Yin, is talking about his math class. "The teacher doesn't care if I go late or not. He never says anything when we go late. He just ignores us. I'll smoke another cigarette before I go." He reaches over and picks up Mary's cigarettes and takes one. Yin Lee takes out his calculator and begins to do his homework. "Hey Yin," says Mourad, "that's a neat calculator. How much did it cost?" "$20.00." Mourad sits up and leans toward Yin closely, "You paid too much, you should have gone to a place I know. $20.00 is too much." He shakes his head. Mary says, "I think I'll get some more coffee. Anybody want anything?" "Yeah, get me some gum," says Maria. Mary walks away.
4. Analyze your own adjustment into American culture using the model on page 19. Give specific examples for each of the steps. Include anything that you did that helped you move from one stage to another.

FOR MORE INFORMATION ABOUT STEREOTYPES:

BRISLIN, R. W., *Cross-cultural Encounters: Face to Face Interaction.* New York: Pergamon Press, 1981.
WITKIN, H. A., and J. W. BERRY, "Psychological Differentiation in Cross-cultural Perspective," in *Journal of Cross-Cultural Psychology* 6, 1975, pp. 4–87.

FOR MORE INFORMATION ABOUT AMERICAN/TEXAN CULTURE:

BELLAH, R. N., R. MADSEN, W. M. SULLIVAN, A. SWINDLER, and S. M. TIPTON, *Habits of the Heart: Individualism and Commitment in American Life.* Berkeley, CA: University of California Press, 1985.
MICHENER, JAMES A., *Texas.* New York: Random House, 1985. **An excellent fictional history of Texas.**
MILLER, RAY, *The Eyes of Texas Travel Guides for Houston/Gulf Coast* (1987), *San Antonio/Border* (1979), *Dallas/East Texas* (1988), *Ft. Worth/Brazos Valley* (1981), *Hill Country/Permian Basin* (1982), *Panhandle/Plains* (1982), Houston, Texas: Gulf Publishing Co.
Films: "Hud," "The Last Picture Show."
Video: "Lonesome Dove."

Chapter 6

Mining Culture Bumps

Up to this point, we have examined the negative consequences of culture bumps: stereotypes, alienation, and the death of curiosity about other people. Both Abdul Aziz and Brian experienced culture bumps without being cognizant of exactly what happened. Each reacted in his particular way and talked about his experiences with people from his own culture. Each, as a result, felt disappointed in himself and in the other person. Each also drew a conclusion or formed a stereotype about the people in the other culture.

Abdul Aziz believes that he "understands" American culture. Brian believes that he "understands" Saudi culture. Therefore, neither one feels that he needs to learn more about the other culture. Their minds are made up. There is no need for further investigation. What has not developed for either of them is a real awareness and appreciation for his own culture or for the other culture.

Let us now explore an alternative way to look at culture bumps. The first step is to recognize the differences that we notice. Each difference is a culture bump.

While we cannot analyze each one, we can isolate one for both Abdul Aziz and Brian. Were Abdul to isolate one, he might choose Brian speaking on the phone and not greeting the new arrivals until he finished his conversation. The following step-by-step process produces a result that is quite distinct from the one we have seen. If we take this culture bump and analyze it, it might look this way.

1. *Pinpoint the culture bump.*

I had a culture bump with a/an _____American_____.
                                     (culture)

They _____talked on the phone and **ignored** my guests_____ and

I thought that was _____**rude**_____.

In step 1, it is important to be specific. Choose an incident that happened and try to remember it as specifically as possible. Even if the same thing has happened repeatedly, isolate one time with which to work.

2. *Define the situation.*

The other person(s) was/were _____male_____.
                                     (male/female)

We were at _____my apartment_____.
                             (location)

The universal situation was _____how a guest in someone's home behaves

when other guests arrive.

It is important to be specific about the situation. It may include the relationship with the other person, if they were older or younger, male or female, stranger, friend, family, and so on. The location is also important. Did the incident happen in public, in private? The situation should be a universal one. People are guests in cultures all over the world but how a guest behaves **varies** from one culture to another. The behavior is **conceptual,** just as a greeting is conceptual. People from cultures all over the world greet one another but how and what they do varies from one culture to another.

3. *List the other's behavior.*

   The other person _____ talked on the phone for five minutes, hung up _____ .
                                    (action verb)

   Review p. 8 on observable behavior. There should be no judgmental observation here, only observable behavior.

4. *List your own behavior.*

   I (was)_____ said, "Welcome, come in" Poured a cup of _____
                                    (action verb)

   coffee for Ziad and Nabil and said, "How are you." I looked at Brian three times.

   Again, list only observable behavior. Your behavior may be only observing. Speaking is considered a behavior.

5. *List your own feelings.*

   At the time I felt _____ surprised, angry, embarrassed and humiliated. _____

   Surprise or shock is usually the initial feeling in a culture bump. You may have several feelings, some good and some bad. Do not write about the other person such as he made me angry or I felt he was rude. Those are thoughts, not feelings.
        In this case one doesn't attempt to guess the feelings of the other. Although, in reality, we frequently ascribe feelings to the other, such as he didn't care, he was cold, he was stiff, he was nosey, he was pushy, and so on.

These first five steps complete the personal part of the process. The next steps help you to understand your culture better and to give you the questions to ask to begin to understand the other culture.

6. *What are your expectations in your own culture?*

   When people in my culture are in the situation defined in step 2

   When Saudis are guests in someone's home and other guests arrive
   (List the situation written in step 2 here.)

   they behave like this: take a moment from talking on the phone to greet the new

   guests and then return to their phone call.
   (List observable behavior here.)

Simply copy what you have written in step 2 in the first line with the name of your culture filled in. On the second line, list only observable behavior, not judgmental behavior such as they are polite.

7. *What is the **underlying** value behind those expectations?*

When people in my culture do <u>take a moment from talking on the phone to greet</u>

<u>the new guests and then return to their phone call</u> ;

(Write behavior listed in step 6 here.)

I say they are _____<u>considerate</u>_____.

Simply copy what you have written on the second line in step 6 on the first line here. The second line will be a concept, such as responsible, polite, friendly, appropriate, and so on.

8. *How do other cultures show that value(s)?*

How do people in <u>American</u> culture show _____<u>consideration</u>_____ ?
                                    (value in step 7)

Write the name of the culture with whom you had the bump in the first blank. Write the word or words that you wrote in the second half of step 7 in the second blank.

        This question gives you a beginning to understand the other culture. You are now asking, "How are they the same as I am?"

9. *How do other cultures behave in the situation defined in step 2?*

<u>Americans complete their conversation and then greet the new guests</u> .

You have now identified a universal situation and then described the behavior of two cultures within that situation.

10. *Why do people in my culture do those things in that way?*

This is an opportunity to reflect on where your cultural behaviors come from.

        Brian , after describing Abdul Aziz as being too formal and **rigid,** changes once he isolates his culture bump and analyzes the incident of Abdul Aziz greeting him. He then would define this situation as how a host greets a guest when both are university-age males. He would describe Abdul Aziz's behavior as shaking his hand, saying "Welcome, it is good to see you," pointing to the sofa, handing him a **demitasse** with Turkish coffee, saying, "How is your family? Are you fine?" He would describe his own behavior as taking Abdul Aziz's hand, saying "Hello," sitting down, responding "Fine, thanks," drinking the coffee and saying, "Hey, man, you got any chips?" He then lists his feelings as surprised, awkward, and embarrassed.

By learning to recognize, name, and analyze our culture bumps, we have the possibility for discovery about ourselves and others. This discovery forms the basis for acceptance and respect between peoples of the world.

A simplified version of the culture bump process follows:

THE CULTURE BUMP

A *culture bump* occurs when a person has expectations of a particular behavior and gets something different when interacting with individuals from another culture.

1. Pinpoint sometime when I have felt different or noticed something different when with someone from another culture.
2. Define the situation.
3. List the behaviors of the other person.
4. List my own behavior.
5. List my feelings in the situation.
6. List the behaviors I expect from people in my own culture in the situation defined in step 2.
7. When people in my culture do the behaviors listed in step 6, I say that they are
   _____.
8. How do people of the other culture express the quality named in step 7?
9. How do people of the other culture behave in the situation listed in step 2?
10. Reflect on the underlying value in my culture that prompts the behavior listed in step 6.

Vocabulary Words

1. **consequences**—results
2. **alienation**—feeling of being separate and isolated
3. **alternative**—different choice
4. **isolate**—separate from the rest
5. **ignored**— not paid attention to
6. **rude**—not polite
7. **varies**—is different
8. **conceptual**—theoretical, ideas
9. **underlying**—hidden, deep
10. **rigid**—stiff
11. **demitasse**—small cup

Choose one of the preceding vocabulary words and place it in the appropriate blank.

1. This plan is not practical; it is too _____ for our use.

2. Since this plan cannot be used, we need to choose an _____ one.

3. I only had a _____ of tea last night.

4. That man shouting at us was very _____.

5. We need to _____ the sick cow from the rest of the herd so that they don't get sick also.

6. I made an A in the course; that is the _____ of studying so hard.

7. He is very depressed. He has strong feelings of _____ from the rest of the class.

8. Although he appears to be very confident, he has _____ feelings of inferiority.

9. The drinking age _____ from state to state.

10. Although the children shouted at the old lady, she _____ them and continued to walk down the street.

11. The arm of the soldier giving a salute was very _____.

Exercise for Step 5

Generate a list of feelings that all human beings have, i.e., love, hate, fear. Use this list when you fill in step 5 on the worksheet.

Form groups of people from similar cultures. Discuss the list of three culture bumps that you made on page 49. Notice how the mirroring process works in your group. Complete the following culture bump worksheet for a culture bump that you have personally experienced. Make extra copies for other culture bumps.

1. Pinpoint the culture bump.

   I had a culture bump with a/an _____
                                                    (culture)

   They did _____

   and I thought that was _____ .
2. *Define the situation.*

   The other person(s) _____ .
                                              (male/female)

   We were at _____ .
                                    (location)

   The situation was _____
3. *List the other's behavior.*

   The other person _____ .
                                           (action verb)
4. *List your own behavior.*

   I _____ .
                                    (action verb)
5. *List your own feelings.*

   At the time I felt _____ .
6. *What are your expectations in your own culture?*
   When people in my culture are in the situation defined in step 2

   _____ ,
                         (List the situation written in step 2 here.)

   they behave like this: _____
                                    (List observable behavior here.)
7. *What is the underlying value behind those expectations?*

   When people in my culture do _____ ,
                                    (Write behavior listed in step 6 here.)

   I say they are _____
8. *How do other cultures show that value(s)?*

   How do people in _____ culture show _____?
                                                          (value in step 7)
9. *How do other cultures behave in the situation defined in step 2?*

   _____

10. *Why do people in my culture do those things in that way?*

    _____

Chapter 7

Nobuhito Tanaka

This story is seen from the point of view of Nobuhito, an older businessman from Japan who studies with the other students because his company has sent him to the university. It takes place on the beach where the students in the cross-cultural communication class are having a picnic. As the story begins, Nobuhito has wandered away from the group. As you read, notice the differences in the communication styles between Nobuhito and Brian, the American. How many different ways are there in which people can communicate?

Non-English Words that Appear in the Story "Tanaka Nobuhito: Japan"

San – Mr., Mrs., or Miss
gaijin – foreigners
karaoke – typical bar which has music tapes

TANAKA NOBUHITO: JAPAN

The brisk cold wind blowing off the ocean felt good on Tanaka Nobuhito's face. It brought a flush to his copper skin and **ruffled** his straight black hair. He placed his walking shoes carefully on a rock and rubbed his toes in the coarse sand. He rolled up the cuffs of his gray slacks and fastened his matching gray windbreaker over his black turtleneck sweater. With his hands clasped behind him, he looked much younger (at least to American eyes) than his 31 years. He took a deep breath and walked slowly down the beach away from his companions who were having a late autumn picnic. Tanaka-*San* had many things **to sort out** that overcast day.

When his company, The Yokohama Corporation, had given him the overseas assignment, he had felt the responsibility deeply. His company had carefully **groomed** him to come to the United States. They had assigned him to negotiate with Americans ever since he had graduated from Tokyo University nine years before.

He remembered vividly his first encounter with Americans—a sales manager and his two assistants. At their first meeting in the Tokyo office, he and his two colleagues had inwardly **squirmed** under the Americans' direct gaze. He could feel his coworkers' discomfort as the Americans hurried through "small talk" in about ten minutes and began to discuss business. But the greatest embarrassment was yet to come.

It was bad enough that all three Americans spoke freely to the three Japanese in the same friendly way, but then they had spoken to the general manager of Nobuhito's division as though he were at the same level as Nobuhito and his colleagues. And things did not get better.

Nobuhito, knowing that they needed to get to know one another well, had arranged for that same group of Americans to visit restaurants, to visit an inn, to have several afternoons of **golf** at the company's golf course (he and his colleagues, of course, were careful to allow their guests to win). The final day had been carefully planned for the business meeting. However, the Americans had gotten progressively more **irritable,** and the more the Japanese had tried **to smooth things over,** the more irritable the *gaijin* had gotten. The Americans left behind an unsigned contract and **a bad taste in Nobuhito's mouth.** Tanaka-*San* had been learning about Americans for a long time. And the four months that he had been at the university had confirmed his general impression of them as being **brash,** impolite, and probably dirty.

Shortly after he, Yuko, and their four-year-old son, Eiichi, had arrived in the United States, Nobuhito had fallen into a deep **melancholy.** Autumn had always been a romantic time for him, but now the browns and golds of the trees brought him little consolation. He missed going out with his colleagues after work to the *karaoke* where they spent hours eating the many small snacks and drinking. As the liquor warmed their insides, they sang along with the music tapes and deeply enjoyed being together. That deep feeling of closeness was what he had been expecting that time that he, Brian, and Alfredo had gone out for a drink after class. He had relaxed with the first **sip** and soon looked out at Alfredo and Brian through an alcoholic **haze.** But somehow it had not been the same. The next morning he was, of course, in class and nobody could tell that he had drunk a lot the evening before. He was surprised that Alfredo didn't come to class at all and that Brian came late, obviously **hung over,** even making a joke about it to Miss Joy.

His and Yuko's relationship was deep. But even his homelife had become a problem. Yuko lived, isolated, in their suburban home, going to the Japanese Society once a week. Other than cleaning the house and talking with other Japanese wives on the phone, she spent hours sitting by Eiichi's side as he made Japanese characters in big, black strokes. But Nobuhito knew that she missed her life back in Tokyo where she shopped each day for fresh vegetables and cleaned their small apartment. And Eiichi, although they sent him to Japanese school all day on Saturday, still seemed to be much more impressed by **He-Man** cartoons. His language was a **garble** of English and Japanese.

Nobuhito stopped and turned toward the water. He watched a sea gull dip and glide away on an air current. He felt, rather than heard, footsteps running up the beach. He turned to see Brian, his face flushed from the wind, jogging toward him.

"Hey, Nobuhito, how 'bout some company?"

Nobuhito wondered what on earth that meant. He smiled.

"Man, this fresh air is great, huh?"

Nobuhito smiled. As he was thinking of his response, Brian slapped him on the shoulder and said,

"You know Nobu, you're a great guy. I really like you."

Nobuhito smiled. He never knew how to respond to the exaggerated compliments that Americans **showered on** everyone around them.

Brian stopped and blew his nose, then stuffed the handkerchief back in his pocket. Nobuhito wondered how they could carry around a handkerchief which they used over and over. But then that was no worse than washing and rinsing in the same water and wearing their shoes with all the germs on them into the house.

They passed an elderly woman on the beach dressed in bright red pants and top.

"Neat, huh. Reminds me of my grandmother."

Nobuhito smiled and recalled his shock at Yuko's story of overhearing an American tell an old lady, "Oh, how pretty you are," and the old lady said, "Thank you!" Nobu shook his head at the memory.

He was pulled out of his reverie by Brian who touched his shoulder and said,

"Wow, look at that!"

His eyes followed Brian's arm pointing upward. The sun had broken through the gray clouds and rays of red, yellow, and pink exploded across the sky. As the two stood gazing at the brilliant scene, he felt his mind begin to clear. After a while, they walked in silence toward the beckoning fire.

He smiled as strains of a song floated on the wind past him, rekindling the familiar feeling of closeness with this group of **widely divergent** strangers.

Vocabulary Words

1. **ruffled**—disarrange
2. **sort out**—examine in order to understand
3. **groomed**—prepared
4. **squirmed**—moved because of feeling uncomfortable
5. **golf**—game played with a small ball and stick
6. **irritable**—upset
7. **smooth things over**—make things fine, tranquil
8. **a bad taste in Nobuhito's mouth**—a bad impression
9. **brash**—acting and speaking without thinking
10. **melancholy**—sadness
11. **baffling**—confusing
12. **sip**—small taste
13. **haze**—cloud
14. **hung over**—feel badly because of drinking too much alcohol
15. **showered on**—give freely
16. **He-Man**—popular cartoon character for children
17. **garble**—mixture
18. **rekindled**—feel once again
19. **widely divergent**—very different

Discussion Questions

In small groups, discuss the following questions. Be prepared to share your discussion with the class.

1. When the Americans visited Nobuhito and his colleagues at their office in Tokyo, how did Nobuhito and his colleagues feel?

2. Had Nobuhito begun to change by the end of the story? If so, how?

3. What did you learn about Japanese culture from this reading? What kind of things are important for Japanese? Are these things important in your culture? In American culture?

4. Where is Nobuhito in the cultural adjustment cycle? (See page 19.) Explain your answer.

COMMUNICATING ACROSS CULTURES

The Three Channels of Communicating

The simple definition of communication as "the process in which meaning is transmitted from one or more individuals to one or more other individuals" is accurate. However, communication between people is a complex process. We communicate constantly, yet rarely pay attention to it. Indeed, we are completely unaware of much of our communication. Communication occurs through three basic channels: (1) nonverbal language, (2) paralanguage, and (3) verbal language. (1)

Verbal Language

We are most familiar with verbal language—grammar, vocabulary, pronunciation, reading, and writing. They are traditionally taught in language courses and are easily recognized as communication. The other two channels are not as easily recognized as being communication and are studied much less frequently. (2)

Paralanguage

Paralanguage includes voice intonation, intensity, speed, silence, and stress. We can readily see how meaning shifts when the paralanguage cues change:

1. Come in. (spoken in a matter of fact, even voice)
2. Come in. (spoken in a loud, rapid, angry tone)
3. Come in. (spoken as a question in a soft, timorous voice)
4. Come in. (spoken in a low, suggestive voice)

The importance that paralanguage plays in the communicative process is apparent. (3)

Nonverbal Language

The third communication channel is nonverbal and includes such things as gestures, posture, facial expressions, eye contact, the use of space, or even our dress. Ray

Birdwhistle in his article "The Language of the Body" says that more than 60% of the social meaning of conversation between Americans is nonverbal.* Posture tells us much. For example, when shoulders are slumped, it can mean that the person is fatigued or defensive. Eye contact, the amount of time one person looks into the eyes of another person, is another important way of communicating. Our distance from someone, touching someone—all these behaviors communicate. Students tell the teacher, "We're tired" or "We're interested" or "We're bored" without saying a word. And our nonverbal behavior, because it is largely unconscious, tends to reflect our true feelings. For example, if a student is saying, "I really enjoy your class" but the student's body is saying, "I'm bored," the teacher will know that the student is bored. (4)

Difference Between the Channels

A significant difference between verbal language and paralanguage or nonverbal language is that we feel comfortable in asking a person to repeat what he or she said if we don't understand his or her words. We almost never ask a person what he or she meant by a behavior that is different. We readily say, "Excuse me, can you repeat that. I didn't understand what you meant." But rarely do we say, "Excuse me, what did you mean by that smile just now? I didn't understand what it meant." (5)

Models of Communication

Let us look more closely at what happens when we communicate. The following is a simple model of the communication process:

Sender sends a>>>(Message)>>>>>> to Receiver who sends a >>> Response (or Message) to>>>> the Receiver(original sender) who sends a>>>> >>> >>>>>>>> (Message) or response>>>>> etc.

Furthermore, one of three things always happens when we communicate:

Sender

Receiver—Message received and interpreted correctly
Receiver—Message not received
Receiver—Message received and misinterpreted

Communication cues are very complex and involved, even within the same culture. (6)

Cross Cultural Miscommunication

To understand cues cross culturally becomes even more complicated because each of us learns the cues that are appropriate in our culture, and each culture has different

*Birdwhistle, Ray, "The Language of the Body" *Human Communication: Theoretical Explorations* edited by Albert Silverstein, Lawrence Erlbaum Assoc. 1974, pp. 213–214.

"cues" to show basic ideas. For example, a Japanese, quickly sucking in his breath, indicates to another Japanese that he is thinking. However, to an American, this same action indicates anger, surprise, or disbelief and, occasionally, thinking. The American usually shows that he is thinking by nodding his head, saying "hmmm," narrowing his or her eyes or similar gestures. So the situation is the same (telling the other person that you are thinking) but if the Japanese does this with an American, the American can misunderstand the cue, causing, at the least, confusion and, at the most, a serious problem. (7)

When Nobuhito and his colleagues met with the American sales representatives, both sides were sending and receiving messages with all three channels. The eye contact was nonverbal, the friendly tone was paralanguage, and the words spoken were verbal. Further, Nobuhito and his coworkers were making unconscious assumptions about the Americans: they like them, they dislike them, they trust them, they distrust them, all based primarily on their nonverbal and paralinguistic behavior. (8)

Similarly, Edward T. Hall in *The Hidden Dimension* says that in public, an American shows that he or she has an intimate relationship with someone by the use of space, by being 6 to 18 inches from the other person (Hall, p. 117). A Latin American can show friendship by using space in the same way and might show an intimate relationship by frequency of contact rather than the simple use of space. A white American shows frankness and openness by direct eye contact while a black American can show respect by lack of eye contact. A white American might show respect by "giving" space to the other individual. In these cross-cultural communication situations, the participants are not giving the meaning that they think they are giving and the other participants are not receiving the meaning that they think they are receiving. Many culture bumps occur when individuals don't know the paralanguage or nonverbal cues of another language. (9)

These culture bumps lead to the white American thinking that the black American is shifty and the black American thinking that the white American is aggressive. The North American thinks that two Latin American friends are lovers and the Latin American thinks that North Americans are cold. The Japanese thinks that Americans "jump to conclusions" and the Americans think that Japanese are untrustworthy. (10)

Different Styles of Communication in Different Cultures

The first step in breaking this cycle of miscommunication is to learn to observe behavior in ourselves and in others. Once we do this, we can begin to define different cultural styles of communication. In order to do this, let us examine several different communication styles. (11)

Looping Styles

Many cultures, such as Saudi, have "loops" at the beginning of conversations. The pattern looks like this:

OOOOOOOOOOOOOOOOX
Hello
How are you?
How are your mother and father?
How is your class?
It is nice to see you.
By the way, I want to talk to you about . . .

American culture, in contrast, has a pattern like this:

OXOOO
Hi.
Listen, I need to talk to you about . . .
By the way, how are your classes?

The "small talk" at the beginning of the conversation is very "big talk" to Arabs while it is "a waste of time" for the American. (12)

High-Context and Low-Context Styles

Still another difference in style of communication is that between high-context and low-context cultures. High-context cultures, like the Japanese, "feel" how other people are. They use all the cues, and rely on their "gut instincts." Americans, a low-context culture, rely much more on verbal messages and written communications. If faced with conflicting messages, they will place great emphasis on verbal messages. Nobuhito, in arranging for the Americans and Japanese to "be together" and get to know one another is operating from both high context and the OOOOOOOOOX pattern of communication. The Americans' irritation came from not being able to operate from their models. Both sides were, of course, unconscious of where their reactions came from and were misjudging the other side. (13)

Silent Styles

Some cultures, such as the Japanese, use silence much more than do Western or Middle Eastern cultures. Japanese can wait for up to 20 seconds comfortably in silence, while Westerners become uncomfortable after only about 7 seconds. Therefore, when an American teacher asks a Japanese a question, the Japanese may take more time to process his or her answer than the American is accustomed to waiting. Americans and others sometimes "jump in" and finish sentences for Japanese and other Asians. The Asian's silence may be misinterpreted as unwillingness to answer or not knowing the answer. On the other hand, the Westerner's "chattiness" may be misinterpreted as foolishness by the Asian. (14)

Successful Cross-Cultural Communication

Once we become aware of different styles of communication in different cultures, we lessen our habit of forming value judgments without knowing why we do so. So the Latin American moves from saying, "Americans are cold people" to "Americans use space differently than I do" to "Americans show friendship in a different way than I do." He may then make a value judgment of "I'm comfortable (or uncomfortable) in that situation." The emphasis changes from they to I. (15)

This process will give you the chance to stop and say, "Why did you smile just then?" Or more importantly, "Why did I notice that smile just now?" And then to ask the most important question, "If I smile in order to be friendly, how do you show friendliness in your culture?" (16)

Comprehension Questions

Put an F by those statements that are false and a T by those that are true. Rewrite the false statements so that they are true.

____ 1. We are usually aware of all the ways in which we communicate.

____ 2. Verbal communication accounts for most of the communication process in English.

____ 3. Sometimes we do not communicate.

____ 4. To understand nonverbal language and paralanguage in another culture is just as important as understanding the grammar and vocabulary of that culture's language.

____ 5. In the example of Nobuhito and the American sales representatives, it was the fault of the Japanese that effective communication did not take place.

____ 6. Misunderstanding of the nonverbal or paralanguage cues of another language can lead to stereotypes of the people from that linguistic background.

____ 7. One of the first steps in breaking cross-cultural miscommunication is observing behavior and defining different styles of communication.

____ 8. The communication style which loops more at the beginning of a conversation shows more sincerity than the style that goes immediately to the point.

_____ 9. Low-context cultures, such as American, do not have highly developed feelings.

_____ 10. In effective cross-cultural communication, the individual examines his or her own reaction rather than judging the other person.

Vocabulary Words

You can frequently guess the meaning of a word by reading the sentences around it. Find the paragraph in the essay on pages 75–79 with the same number as the number in the parentheses. Then find the word that fits the definition and write it in the blank.

Example:

(Paragraph 1) Means _____ *channel* _____

(Paragraph 1) Connected series of action _____

(Paragraph 1) Complicated _____

(Paragraph 1) A part of the communication process _____

(Paragraph 1) Any part of communication that uses words _____

(Paragraph 3) Easily _____

(Paragraph 3) Fearful _____

(Paragraph 3) Sexy _____

(Paragraph 4) The way we hold our body _____

(Paragraph 4) Tired _____

(Paragraph 4) Looking in another's eyes _____

(Paragraph 4) Without thinking _____

(Paragraph 7) Fitting, suitable _____

(Paragraph 7) Inhale through the mouth _____

(Paragraph 8) Expectation _____

(Paragraph 10) Untrustworthy _____

(Paragraph 14) Talking a lot _____

Word Forms

In English, sometimes the noun form of a word is the same as the verb form. Choose the correct word form to fit into the following sentences. Write the part of speech at the end of each sentence (verb or noun).

Example:
to process, process

1. The admission ____process____ is complicated. *(N)*

2. The admission officer ____processed____ my papers quickly. *(V)*

to channel, channel

1. He _____ his money through a bank in the Bahamas. (   )

2. That television _____ went off the air last week. (   )

to fatigue, fatigue

1. His _____ showed in his face. (   )

2. Skiing always _____ me. (   )

to contact eyes, eye contact

1. He has very direct _____. (   )

2. The wife tried to_____ her husband's _____ during the party.
   (   )

to chat, chat

1. The neighbors _____ every day. (   )

2. Joan and I had a nice _____. (   )

Communication Exercises

Show the nonverbal behavior for each of the following ideas. Notice the differences between different cultures. How might these differences affect interpersonal relations?

Come here.
Good-bye.
Shame on you.
Count to 10 (using your fingers).
OK.

In small groups, draw up a list of characteristics that would help an individual to communicate across cultures more effectively. For example,

1. a sense of humor
2. understanding something about the other person's background

Crossword Vocabulary Review

Using the vocabulary words listed on pages 43, 44, 46, 47, 53, 56, 57, 67, 74, and 81, fill in the blanks in the puzzle.

ACROSS
1. Results
3. Neither good nor bad
5. Game played with a small ball and stick
7. Small taste
9. Connection
11. Quickly
13. Unintentionally
14. Without much furniture
15. To speak slowly

DOWN
1. To make sure, give proof
2. Bad
4. Fearful
6. Material
8. A flat metal ornament hung on the wall
10. To speak informally about unimportant things
12. Any part of communication that uses words

Answer to crossword puzzle on page 83.

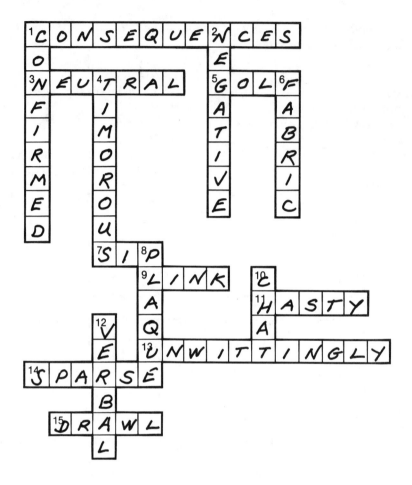

For More Information about Cross-Cultural Communication:

Barnlund, Dean C., *Interpersonal Communication: Survey and Studies.* Boston, MA: Houghton Mifflin, 1968.

Birdwhistle, Ray. "The Language of the Body," *Human Communication: Theoretical Exploration,* Albert Silverstein, ed., Lawrence Erlbaum Assoc., 1974. **Article about the breakdown of the communication process.**

Condon, John and Fathi Yousef, *An Introduction to Intercultural Communication.* Indianapolis, In: Bobbs-Merrill, 1975. **Another classic text.**

Morris, Desmond, et al. *Gestures.* New York: Stein and Day, 1979.

Samovar, Larry A. and Richard E. Porter, *Intercultural Communication: A Reader.* Belmont, CA: Wadsworth Publishing Company, Inc., 1972. **This is a classic textbook for communication across cultures. It includes a great deal of comparative information between Japanese and American cultures.**

THE FOLLOWING REPRESENT ONLY A SMALL PERCENTAGE OF THE WEALTH OF INFORMATION AVAILABLE ABOUT JAPAN.

CLAVELL, JAMES, *Shogun.* New York: Atheneum, 1975. **A well written historical novel.**

CONDON, JOHN, *With Respect to the Japanese.* Yarmouth, Maine: Intercultural Press, 1984.

NAKAMURA, HAJIME, *Ways of Thinking of Eastern Peoples: India—China—Tibet—Japan.* Honolulu, HI: East-West Center Press, 1964.

TSUNODA, RYUSAKU, *Sources of Japanese Tradition.* New York: Columbia University Press, 1958.

Chapter 8

Alfredo Chavez

The story is now seen through the eyes of Alfredo Chavez, a young man from Venezuela. As you read the story, notice the things that are important to Alfredo. See if you can trace the relationship between his values and his behavior. How do your values influence your behavior? Where do Alfredo's values come from? See if you can identify at which stage(s) Alfredo is in the cultural adjustment cycle.

**Non-English Words that Appear in the Reading
"Alfredo Chavez: Venezuela"**

cafe con leche – coffee with milk

palanca – influence, pull

arepas – bread made with corn meal eaten in Venezuela

salsa – a music very popular in Venezuela and other Latin countries

llañero music – "country music" typical of the plains area of Venezuela

Hola, que tal? – hello, how are you?

Bien, y tu – fine and you?

Mas o menos – so so

Universidad Central de Venezuela – a large, public university in Caracas, Venezuela

ALFREDO CHAVEZ: VENEZUELA

He is the youngest of Franklin Alfredo Chavez and Ana Cristina Gonzales de Chavez's six children. Their only son's skin color was a mixture of black from his father and white from his mother called *cafe con leche* in Venezuela. He is called Black in America. Alfredo Chavez moves with an easy grace that is **enhanced** by his open smile. Few Americans, in talking with him, are aware that his mind is busy trying to discover who has influence to ensure his network of *palanca* in this new environment. For Alfredo Chavez has learned well the art of living from his father, vice president of the Venezuelan national oil company, and he knows that success is assured by maintaining a **vast** network of contacts, associates, and friends. One can depend only on one's family and friends; that network of **reciprocal** obligations had worked very well indeed for most of Alfredo's 22 years.

Born and raised in Caracas, Venezuela, Alfredo had always been adored by his older sisters. He finds being the center of attention natural and had assumed his life would continue in the same way here in the United States. For his mother, Ana Cristina, the upper-class daughter of a leading Caraqueña family, he has deep devotion. He now misses intensely the talks they used to share at the kitchen table in the sprawling family home high on the hills overlooking Caracas. In fact, he misses much from back home:

the **streets teeming with people,** the smell of diesel overlaying the shouts and laughter
   that filled the air

the constant **influx of friends** at home—there were always one or two guests at the
   table

groups of friends going dancing only to return home at 6:00 A.M. for a noisy breakfast
   where his mother and father joined the young people for rich hot coffee and
   arepas

and music everywhere, the pulsing rhythm of *salsa*, "modern music," and the haunting strains of *llañero* music.

In a poor imitation of this rich musical heritage, Alfredo keeps a tape recorder going **full blast** in his dorm room. And even though he goes to the discos, he is only getting **warmed up** at 2 A.M. when they close.

Now, after two months, Alfredo is losing his initial excitement at coming to the United States to study. His longing for home deepens as his bewilderment at life in America increases. And, in the mornings, when he wakes, his **mind turns to** the incidents that confuse and anger him. He **turns fitfully** at memories of incidents like the time he overheard Kathy asking Luz Maria if she were going out with that Black guy from Venezuela. Brian had laughed, puzzled, when Alfredo had asked him who the Black guy from Venezuela was.

He sulked when the teacher **rebuked** him for talking to Luz Maria in class,

"You might try paying as much attention to your homework as you do to girls."

But he knew he wasn't studying. It seemed impossible to sit at the desk in his room and concentrate; something would drive him out or he would sit for hours with *salsa* **blaring** from his headphones. His conversations with Julio now are frequently about Americans—how cold they are, how they don't know how to have a good time, how stupid they are, "look how they stand in lines for everything—like cows—even for red lights, how terrible the food is and always, always, back home . . ."

But, with no one did he touch on the cold fear deep inside that he wouldn't make it, that he'd have to return home a failure. Even deeper was his sadness at the **shattering** of his dream of a warm and welcoming America and Americans that he had always carried in his head.

Alfredo Chavez rises late, showers and dresses—neatly pressed, faded blue jeans, a **starched** white shirt, open, revealing a gold chain on his brown chest and black Italian-style loafers. He grabs his books and passes by the cafeteria (how can they eat all that food in the morning?!). He remembers his conversation with Brian, "I never knew I was Black till I came to America," he thinks. His thoughts are interrupted by Julio.

"Hola, que tal?"
"Bien, y tu?"
"Mas o menos."
They shake hands.
"Do you have the homework?"
"No, do you?"
"No, hey, there's Nobuhito. Let's ask him."
"Hey, Nobu, do you have the homework?"
"Thanks!"

The boys copy the neatly printed homework and rush off to class.

In class, Alfredo lounges in a chair and attempts to follow Joy Taylor's explanation about patterns of communication. He **spirits soar** when Joy laughs at his explanation that he would kiss any woman who **slapped** him in public, even though he hadn't meant it as a joke. Luz Maria's smile is encouraging; he enjoys **flirting** with her, an elaborate game of "come to me, go from me" that he had learned early from watching his sisters. An acknowledged sexuality permeated all male/female exchanges in Venezuela, and he now found Americans with their determination to treat one another as equals to be curiously colorless.

He goes to the cafeteria for lunch with Julio, Alberto, and Carlos. Standing in line, the boys look long and admiringly at several American girls walking past. They laugh loudly to cover their embarrassment when one girl spits out,

"What's your problem, jerks!"

Alfredo has soup, meat, vegetables, rice, beer, and then a cup of coffee. Watching the Americans around him, Alfredo wonders at the numbers who sit alone, reading a book as they eat a hamburger and drink milk—of all things! But, his attention is quickly brought back to the group, as other Latins come by, stop, shake hands, kiss one another on the cheek, talk a bit, or sit down and smoke a cigarette and drink a cup of coffee. Their table is a focal point with people constantly coming and going, numerous conversations going on at the same time at a level that breaks the concentration of the Americans around. And Alfredo feels a deep contentment, being a part of the group, knowing them and being known—a contentment that evaporates when he realizes it is 1:20 and his class began at 1:00.

He gathers his books, says good-bye, and walks across campus to class. He notices a girl with long, blonde hair walking toward him and an image of walking across campus at the *Universidad Central de Venezuela* flashes through his mind. The girl, always aware of the boy looking at her, the split second that their eyes meet, the girl looking away, and him staring intensely at her, whispering a sweet greeting, knowing that she heard and expected it—a ritual satisfying to both. Then **superceding that image,** the American girl's face, angry, "What's your problem, jerks!"

Alfredo lowers his eyes and thinks of December when he can go home again, home to the smell of black beans and rice being cooked by Estella, the Dominican cook, **mingled** with the perfume of his sisters as they dress to go out, his mother's hair, the elegant women, the parties where families dance, the children learning the sensual movements of tropical music from parents, and older brothers, and sisters. And the sound of *salsa* everywhere; its mixture of jazz, African, and Spanish reflecting the **myriad** of cultures and races that merge in the flowing **pulsing** humanity of Venezuela. Little does Alfredo dream that the Christmas trip home will be the lever that enables him to begin his successful sojourn in the United States.

Vocabulary Words

1. **shock of black hair**—lots of black hair
2. **enhanced**—made better
3. **vast**—huge
4. **reciprocal**—mutual
5. **streets teeming with people**—streets filled with people
6. **influx of friends**—lots of friends coming to the house
7. **full blast**—very loud
8. **warmed up**—getting started

9. **mind turns to**—thinks about
10. **turns fitfully**—tosses and turns uncomfortably
11. **rebuked**—reprimanded, admonished
12. **blaring**—very loud
13. **shattering**—breaking (as in breaking a glass)
14. **starched**—stiff
15. **spirits soared**—felt very happy
16. **slapped**—hit on the face with an open palm
17. **flirting**—romantic playing at courtship
18. **spit out**—say very angrily
19. **superceding that image**—covering up that image
20. **mingling**—mixing
21. **myriad**—many kinds
22. **pulsing**—throbbing, beating

Discussion Questions

In small groups, discuss the following questions. Be prepared to share your discussion with the class.

1. Why was Alfredo afraid?

2. What effect did his experience with the American girl have on him? How do you think he feels about American girls?

3. It has been said that black is a color in Venezuela while Black is a culture in the United States. What are the advantages to each of these points of view?

4. What are the stages of cultural adjustment that you can identify in the reading? Give specific examples to explain each stage (page 19).

PEOPLE WHO LIVE IN GLASS CULTURES*

Alfredo's painful sojourn in the United States underscores a fundamental assumption that we make about ourselves. We assume that culture is something that we are rather than understanding that it is only one aspect of our identity. (1)

*People who live in glass houses should not throw stones.

Human Beings Versus Individual Beings Versus Cultural Beings

Perhaps a more accurate way to describe ourselves might be as human beings who are born with individual characteristics and have acquired cultural characteristics. We assume that we are born a Japanese, or an American, or a Venezuelan rather than realizing that we are born a human being into a particular culture and our individual characteristics are molded within that cultural context. For example, if an American were dropped in Caracas five minutes after being born, we readily accept that he would speak Spanish. Yet, we rarely think that he would also have Venezuelan culture. He would, indeed, "be Venezuelan." (2)

It is difficult to assess which parts of our personality, of our belief system, and of our ideas are cultural and which are individual. Yet once we begin to distinguish ourselves as cultural beings, individual beings, and universal beings, we can sort out our reactions to others with more accuracy. (3)

Cultural Values

Since culture plays such an important role in determining our personality and our belief system, it behooves us to understand what makes one cultural context differ from another. If we examine the list of cultural values on page 96, we notice that these values exist in all cultures. However, they receive more emphasis in one culture than in other cultures or perhaps they are interpreted as negative in one culture and as positive in another culture. When they receive emphasis, they are termed a *cultural value* for that particular culture. (4)

Cultural Behavior

The second aspect of culture is the cultural behavior. The cultural values determine the form of behavior in any universal situation in a cyclical form. An Algerian wedding is an example of this cultural cycle. The universal situation of party or celebration is interpreted within the cultural value of men and women being separate, which leads to the cultural behavior of separate men and women's parties at traditional weddings. (5)

A model of this cycle might look like this:

The value of men and women being separate *leads to*

      separate parties for men and women at a wedding *which reinforces*

the value of men and women being separate *which leads to*

separate coffee houses for men and women *which reinforces*

the value of men and women being separate *which leads to*

separate living rooms for men and women *which . . .(etc)*

Cultural Generators

This cycle acts as a generator with the universal concepts being expressed through behaviors that are manifestations of particular cultural values. In the preceding example, separate parties for men and women come from the value that says that men and women are separate and the behavior reinforces the value, and so on. (6)

Comprehension Questions

Put an F by those statements that are false and a T by those that are true. Rewrite the false statements so that they are true.

____ 1. We are our culture.

____ 2. We would be exactly the way we are even if we had been born in another country.

____ 3. The title of the article means that it is best not to criticize other cultures since one's own culture is also vulnerable to criticism.

____ 4. We can understand others better if we understand which parts of ourselves are cultural, individual, and human.

____ 5. We usually think our cultural belief is universal.

____ 6. Cultural behaviors are logical if we know the values from which they spring.

____ 7. The more a people practice a particular behavior the more that behavior will reinforce the value on which it is based.

____ 8. There is no relation between behavior and value in culture.

____ 9. The title of the article means that no one culture has the "truth."

____10. Algerians don't know how to really have fun because they have separate parties for men and women.

Vocabulary Words

Following are definitions to words that are used in the essay on pages 91–93. Find the word in the paragraph number next to the definition. Write the correct word in the blank next to its definition.

Example:

(Paragraph 1) To stay temporarily _____ *To sojourn* _____

(Paragraph 2) To get, to obtain _____

(Paragraph 2) To form, to shape _____

(Paragraph 3) To evaluate, to judge   _____

(Paragraph 4) To be essential, necessary _____

(Paragraph 4) An idea important in a culture _____

(Paragraph 5) Activity influenced by one's culture _____

(Paragraph 6) Something that makes things work, causes _____

(Paragraph 6) To make stronger, emphasize _____

Vocabulary Exercise

Fill in the blanks with vocabulary words listed on pages 91, 92, and 94. The answers follow.

1. The electrical _____ blew up last night so we have no electricity today.

2. The sculptor _____ the statue from clay.

3. The Atlantic Ocean is a _____ expanse of water.

4. In the springtime, there are a _____ of flowers of all colors in the country-side.

5. I couldn't sleep last night because my neighbors were playing their radio _____.

6. Individualism is a strong _____ in American culture.

7. The window was _____ when the kid hit a baseball through it.

8. I was so scared that I could feel my blood _____ through my veins.

9. The girl was so angry that she _____ the man on the face before she could stop herself.

10. The tax office will _____ the amount of money that each person must pay each year in taxes.

1. generator 2. molded 3. vast 4. myriad 5. full blast 6. cultural value 7. shattered 8. pulsing 9. slapped 10. assess

Word Forms

In English, many times the noun form of a verb will end with -ment, -or, or -tion. Choose the correct word form to fit into the following sentences. Write the part of speech at the end of each sentence (verb or noun).

Example:
to sojourn, sojourner

1. *We will* _____*sojourn*_____ *in the south of France. (verb)*

2. *He was a* _____*sojourner*_____ *in our small town. (noun)*

to acquire, acquisition

1. That was an expensive _____. (   )

2. Next year, we will _____ another painting. (   )

to assess, assessment

1. My _____ of the situation was accurate. (   )

2. We need _____ the situation. (   )

to generate, generator

1. We use an electric _____ in our cabin. (   )

2. The river _____ lots of power. (   )

to manifest, manifestation

1. His attitude is a _____ of his inferiority complex. (   )

2. Fear sometimes _____ itself as anger. (   )

to reinforce, reinforcement

1. We gave the child candy as _____ for good behavior. (   )

2. We _____ the child for acting nicely. (   )

Values	
American	**Contrast American**
1. Doing, progress, change striving external achievement	"Being," fatalistic, spontaneity
2. Fast, busy life	Steady, rhythmic, noncompulsive life
3. Individual responsibility	Group responsibility
4. Identity in self	Identity in role, group, family, society, clan
5. People being affected make decisions	Proper authorities make decisions
6. Rely on self and impersonal organizations	Rely on superiors, patron, group
7. Planning to solve problems	Coping to solve problems
8. Student-centered learning	Passive students, rote learning
9. Equality, informality	Hierarchial, formality
10. Sex equality, friends of both sexes	Distinct, male or female superior, friends of same sex
11. Society controls by guilt	Society controls by shame
12. Social friendship	Intense friendship
13. Motivated by achievement	Motivated by ascription
14. Competition is good	Competition is not acceptable
15. Man's nature is changeable	Man's nature is fixed
16. Good health and material comfort is expected	Some disease and material misery is natural
17. Time is future oriented, limited in precise units, linear	Time is past or present oriented not limited, undifferentiated, circular
18. Private property is extension of self	Property is to be used regardless of ownership

Based on a list of cultural values in *Intercultural Sourcebook* by David S. Hoopes and Paul Ventura, published by Intercultural Network, Inc., pp. 48–51.

CULTURAL MODELS

The following two models of culture developed by Pierre Cass* show another way of contrasting American cultural values with those of other cultures.

*Pierre Cass, *Training for the Cross Cultural Mind, A Handbook for Cross Cultural Trainers and Consultants* Society for Intercultural Education, Training and Research, Washington, D.C., 1980, p. 48.

Stairstep Model of Cultural Reality   ## Roller-Coaster Model of Cultural Reality

In the stairstep model (which typifies many American values), the individual begins at the bottom and by hard work, moves up. The beliefs associated with this model are that individuals have control of their lives, individuals are responsible for their lives and that upward striving is desirable. The individual in this model would be competitive and ambitious. In contrast, in the roller-coaster model, outside forces control the individual, the individual has minimal control over his or her life. There is an emphasis on enjoyment of the present and it doesn't matter how hard the individual works. There is only certainty of peaks and valleys in succession in the future.

Values Clarification Exercises

Discuss the following questions.

Does your culture predominantly fit the staircase or the roller-coaster model?
Can you think of examples when this has caused cultural misunderstandings with other cultures?
What skills would people raised in each of the models develop?

Go through the list of cultural values on page 96 and circle those values that are dominant in your culture. You may find some on the right side and some on the left side or they may be equally emphasized in your culture. Go through the list again, placing an X by your personal values. What do you notice?

Based on the values that you have circled, complete the following worksheet.

List a cultural value that is dominant in your culture.

_____

List a behavior that results from the value listed previously.

_____

List a second behavior that results from the value listed previously.

_____

List a second cultural value that is dominant in your culture.

_____

List a behavior that results from the value listed previously.

_____

List a second behavior that results from the value listed previously.

_____

List a value that is considered American.

_____

List a behavior that results from the American value.

_____

List a second behavior that results from the American value.

_____

FOR MORE INFORMATION ABOUT CULTURAL VALUES:

HOOPES, DAVID S. and PAUL VENTURA, *Intercultural Sourcebook.* LaGrange Park, IL: Intercultural Network, Inc., 1979.

KLUCKHOHN, FLORENCE R. and FRED L. STRODTBECK, *Variation in Value Orientations.* New York: Row, Peterson, 1961.

KOHLS, L. ROBERT, *Survival Kit for Overseas Living.* Chicago, IL: Intercultural Press, Inc., 1979, Ch. 7.

ROGERS, CARL H., "Toward a Modern Approach to Values," *Journal of Abnormal and Social Psychology,* 68, no. 2, (1964), 160–167. **An excellent article that tells how one learns values within one's culture and then proposes a new orientation toward values based on one's own experience in life.**

WEEKS, WILLIAM H., PAUL B. PEDERSEN and RICHARD W. BRISLIN, *A Manual of Structured Experiences for Cross Cultural Learning.* Georgetown University,

Washington, D.C., published by Society for Intercultural Education, Training and Research, 1977. **Exercises on value orientation.**
Film: "The Gods Must Be Crazy"

FOR MORE INFORMATION ABOUT VENEZUELA:

BLUTSTEIN, HOWARD I., et. al.,   *Handbook for Venezuela.* 1977. **Area handbook prepared by the Foreign Area Studies of American University in Washington, DC. Has the basic facts about social, economic, political, and military institutions and practices of Venezuela. Available from the Superintendent of Documents, U.S. Printing Office, Washington, DC.**
GALLEGOS, ROMULO, trans. by Robert Malloy,   *Doña Barbara.* Magnolia, MA: Peter Smith Press, 1948. **A novel written by a former president of Venezuela (1945–48) that tells of life on the Venezuelan plains at the turn of the century. A Venezuelan school classic.**
PIETRI, ARTURO ULAR, trans. by Harriet de Onis,   *The Red Lances.* New York: Alfred Knopf, 1963. **A former ambassador to UNESCO tells of the time during the bloody wars of independence and gives an insightful look into the lives and character of the people of the time.**
YBARRA, T. R.,   *Bolivar, the Passionate Warrior.* New York: Ives Washburn, 1929. **An objective account of the life of Simon Bolivar.**

Chapter 9

Phi Thi Vo

The story is now told from the point of view of Phi Thi Vo, who unlike the other students will live in the United States as an immigrant. How is her life different from the lives of the students already introduced in the class? Also notice the difference in how she uses space and how it is used by Americans and the other students. Do people use space differently in your culture than Americans do? If so, how is it different?

Non-English Words that Appear in the Reading "Phi Thi Vo: Vietnam"

ao dais – long dress over black pants worn by Vietnamese women

PHI THI VO: VIETNAM

Taller than the average Vietnamese woman, she keeps her head lowered self-consciously and when she raises it, her wide eyes, slanting upward remind you of fluttering butterflies. If you look closely, you can see light blue veins at the temples beneath her **alabaster** skin. She **glides** soundlessly and speaks softly. None of her classmates, looking at her long delicate fingers folded on her desk, could imagine the fear and horror that **gripped** her stomach during her escape from Ho Chi Minh City or the terror that **propelled** her across the jungles of Vietnam and Cambodia. Nor could they imagine the almost unbearable years in a refugee camp in Thailand. Few could imagine her joy when her maternal uncle brought her to America to live with his wife, Kim Lin, and their two children, Trung and Lien. None could imagine the nightmares she had last night of **grinning** monkeys **slashing** heads. For Phi holds these and other feelings deep inside her.

Phi Thi Vo is beginning to think that maybe this time she can learn English; two years ago when she came to America, it had seemed that English was **beyond her grasp.** She remembered her foolish pride in being first in the English class in the refugee camp and then her **despondence** when, at last in America, she realized she couldn't understand anything!

But by gradually **melding** into the city's Vietnamese community, there had been few times when she had really needed English. She stayed in her aunt and uncle's brick suburban home that looked like all the others—only the shoes on the porch outside the door suggesting the difference in this family. But inside the house, the light pours through the French **lace** curtains and falls on the low black **lacquered** coffee table with its exquisite pink flower arrangement (bought from the Vietnamese nuns at St. Joseph Catholic Church). Brilliant orange and red elongated Vietnamese figures in the painting over the dining room table recall images of Saigon. In the kitchen, where Phi prepares the meals, bits and pieces of Vietnam are everywhere—thin china bowls, chopsticks, heavy glass soup spoons, the packages of thin rice **vermicelli,** the electric rice steamer, jars of fish sauce, jars of lemon grass, thin wooden **skewers** for barbeque and 8# bags of rice. The garden with rows and rows of Asian vegetables and spices can be seen through the kitchen window.

From the outside, the house looks American but life inside the house **approximates** life in Saigon. Here, as there, it is a life that revolves around family.

Phi spends her day taking care of Trung, six, and Lien, four.

There are weekly gatherings of friends when Vietnamese language fills the room. The elegant women wear 3″ heels and **glittering** dresses and the men wear suits with flared legs and shoes with thick heels.

Uncle sits at the head of the table overseeing the many courses. First, crisp Vietnamese egg rolls with thinly sliced cucumbers and fresh cilantro wrapped in lettuce. Then soup, followed by barbequed pork wrapped around wooden skewers, fragrant with lemon grass and garlic. And finally, a whole fish, freshly caught that morning. And of course, the ever present beer and the small saucers of hot fish sauce.

The whole family goes shopping on Saturdays at Vietnam Plaza with its dirty floors, its rows of canned goods imported from Thailand, fresh fish, and shrimp. The tailor, his shop **tucked** in a corner, sits making the black, **baggy** pants and long *ao dais* of the women. Next door to his shop is the Vietnamese hair salon, cluttered with people and Christmas lights which are left up all year long.

On special evenings they go dancing at Tu Do Plaza where the Vietnamese band plays a mixture of punk, tangos, cha chas, and ballads, while the sophisticated singers switch between Vietnamese, French, and Chinese languages. At those dances, Phi sits quietly by Aunt and Uncle, her eyes lifting up to meet the eyes of the **appropriate** men they always invite. Men like Tan, a professor in Vietnam, an insurance salesman in America.

Throughout "Little Saigon" young men sit silently in restaurants, their shirts open, their faces expressionless, their eyes half closed against the smoke from their cigarettes held between the thumb and forefinger. The immigrants have Vietnamese income tax offices, Vietnamese insurance offices, Vietnamese sandwich shops, Vietnamese jewelry shops, Vietnamese coffee shops with rich coffee laced with sweet canned milk—and even Vietnamese gangsters.

But the more it approximates back home, the deeper is the sense of loss of land, loss of families, loss of life—losses that permeate the Vietnamese songs and underlie every conversation. Little Saigon, providing the goods and services to a refugee people ultimately serves as a constant, cruel reminder that this isn't Saigon.

It was almost as big a shock to leave this **hidden cushion** of Vietnamese life and enter the University as it had been to leave her comfortable middle-class home in Saigon. For Phi, the bus ride from Uncle's home to the university is also a voyage into America and she begins to see what Aunt and Uncle and the other Vietnamese had said all along—the untrustworthiness of the Americans (they talk too much), the lack of respect for teachers (students drinking Cokes in class and speaking out), the lack of caring on the part of teachers (never helping students by pointing out all they were doing wrong—how can we know what to do; we're only students!). Phi was also horrified at the couples with their arms around one another, sometimes even kissing, on the bus, on campus. She is amazed at Americans speaking so quickly and so much, without thinking.

At the same time, it is in the class with students from all over the world that she begins to notice something strange. The other Asians view her as "partly" American. She, at first resists the notion, then admits that she has indeed become American in comparison to the newly arrived students. She never forgets that Li Li will one day return to Shanghai and Nobuhito to Tokyo. She will spend the rest of her life here, in this American city, with its imitation Saigon.

Although she would never admit it and can **scarcely bear** to think it, she sometimes wonders if she is losing her Vietnamese culture. Who am I really? Who will my children be? These thoughts cross her mind more and more on the long bus ride as she moves back and forth from one world to another in the space of a day.

Vocabulary Words

1. **temples**—flat space on side of forehead
2. **alabaster**—white and translucent
3. **glide**—move smoothly
4. **gripped**—seized
5. **propelled**—pushed
6. **grinning**—smiling
7. **slashing**—cutting
8. **beyond her grasp**—impossible for her to do or understand
9. **despondence**—depression
10. **meld**—merge
11. **lace**—a special, delicate, thin material
12. **lacquered**—shiny paint
13. **vermicelli**—thin spaghetti
14. **skewers**—long, thin sticks used to cook meat over fire
15. **approximates**—is like
16. **appropriate**—suitable
17. **tucked**—put something snugly
18. **baggy**—loose fitting
19. **hidden cushion**—protected enclave
20. **scarcely bear**—almost cannot tolerate

Discussion Questions

In small groups, discuss the following questions. Be prepared to share your discussion with the class.

1. What are some special problems that an immigrant faces that temporary residents do not?

2. What is "Little Saigon"? Are there similar places in your country? What purpose do they serve?

3. Where are many of the immigrants in the cultural adjustment cycle? Explain your answer. How well adjusted do you think Phi will be five years from now?

SPACE ACROSS CULTURES

Definition of Proxemics

Different cultures have different orientations toward space or proxemics. This difference is reflected in countless situations. For example, when Phi is shocked by young couples embracing on the bus, she is experiencing a cultural difference in proxemics. (1)

Edward T. Hall in *The Hidden Dimension* published by Doubleday and Co., Inc., Garden City, New York in 1966 describes four distance zones that are typical for Americans. They are generalizations and refer specifically to middle-class, white Americans living mostly in the northeastern part of the United States. These distances are typical in normal situations. If the people were angry or excited, or if there were a high noise level or very little light, the distances would change. (2)

Intimate Distance

(Touching to 18 inches, 45.72 centimeters)

This is how close people are to one another when they make love, wrestle, or protect and comfort another person. Some characteristics of this phase are: (1) vision is blurred, (2) arms can reach around the other person, (3) a lot of detail can be seen, (4) the eyes try to cross, (5) one can easily smell the other person and can feel the heat from the other's body. Americans are generally uncomfortable this close to one another in public, although some younger people will be this close. (3)

Personal Distance

(1-1/2 feet or 45.72 centimeters to 4 feet or 1.22 meters)
Hall refers to personal distance as a "small protective sphere or bubble that an organism maintains between itself and others" (Hall, p. 119). If one is in the close phase of personal distance with another person, one can reach out and hold his hand or arm. In the closer phases, only husbands and wives will be this close to one another in public while the farther phases are more appropriate for the distance between friends. People are still close enough to touch; Americans will talk about personal subjects at this distance and try to keep their breath away from the person with whom they are speaking. (4)

Social Distance

(4 feet or 1.22 meters to 12 feet or 3.66 meters)
For Americans, this distance is used between people who are working together. Office mates will use the closer phase and more formal business dealings for the farther phases. Americans will maintain eye contact, moving their eyes from the eyes to the mouth and back again. If you stand up and look down at someone at this distance, the effect is one of domination. The farther phases can also be used as a way of showing authority. To be anywhere within this distance (up to 7 feet) requires acknowledgment of another's presence. (5)

Public Distance

(12 or 3.66 meters to 25 feet or 7.62 meters)

Americans use this distance when they are not closely involved with one another. It is the distance at which you can "run away" easily if needed. You must speak loudly but not shout. It is a distance at which groups interact with one another. In the farther phase, it is the distance that important figures maintain in public (Hall, pp. 116–125).

(6)

Americans and Space

Americans use space in order to show respect or disrespect for one another. A person can "enter" another's space in various ways: (1) by actually physically entering it, (2) through eye contact, (3) by the use of sound. All of these are considered "entering" one's space. The use of space is one of the most important elements of American culture. Americans respond to "misuse" of space in ways that range from discomfort to irritation to anger. The American orientation to proxemics explains why they smile and nod at strangers in public if they make eye contact. To not acknowledge that they have "entered" the other's space could be interpreted as aggressive. Americans are so sensitive to one another's bubble of space that they say "excuse me" if they come within 5 to 11 inches of another person in public. (7)

Proxemics in Different Cultures

Edward C. Stewart in *American Cultural Patterns* says

> confrontation in its most direct form . . . begins when someone **penetrates** the spatial envelope of privacy surrounding each American. When someone draws nearer than about arm's length, the American is likely to interpret this as a sign that he must fight or flee. For this reason the close proximity Latins or Arabs prefer while conversing disturbs Americans since physical nearness carries either a sexual or a belligerent meaning. If the American backs away, then the Latin or Arab may feel that he is being treated with aloofness, if not hostility. In some cultures, however, Thai or Japanese, it is the American who often stands too close during a conversation. The idea of confrontation goes beyond physical displacement. When faced with a problem, Americans like to get to its source. This means facing the facts, meeting the problem head on, putting the cards on the table and getting information "straight from the horse's mouth." It is also desirable to face people directly to confront them intentionally. A contrast to the American values of confrontation is supplied by the indirection of the Japanese or Vietnamese in social matters. (Stewart, 1972, p. 52)

When Brian slapped Nobuhito on the back at the beach and when he was telling him directly what a great guy he thought Nobuhito was, he was "invading" Nobuhito's space. (8)

Hospitality in Different Cultures

Another manifestation of the difference in the use of space can be seen in the concepts of hospitality between different cultures. The American, with his or her emphasis on personal space has the opposite concept of hospitality as the Arab and Vietnamese. For the American it is the guest who is honored by being invited into one's personal space, while in the other two cultures it is the host who is honored by guests coming to his or her home. Phi's uncle rules over the table making sure his guests have more than enough to eat and for Abdul Aziz, it is an honor to have a guest in his home. He is the one honored and his guests (Arabs) make sure that they stay long enough, eat, and drink with him so that he will not be dishonored. However, when Brian was treated royally by Abdul Aziz, he felt uncomfortable since he had already been honored merely by being invited into Abdul's home. (9)

Other Spatial Differences

Other examples of a spatial conflict occur when Luz Maria starts to kiss Joy on the cheek. She remembers that this is not the custom just in time to avert a "culture bump." Nadia, Samira, and Najwa sitting close together and touching are expressing caring in a Middle Eastern way; American girls in the same situation, while expressing caring, would stay out of one another's bubble of space. (10)

Comprehension Questions

Put an F by those statements that are false and a T by those that are true. Rewrite the false statements so that they are true.

_____ 1. Different cultures use space in different ways.
_____ 2. Proxemics refers to physical space.
_____ 3. Arabs are much more hospitable than Americans.
_____ 4. Americans are very friendly because they greet everyone they meet.
_____ 5. In American culture, there are three ways to enter another's space.
_____ 6. If an American can put his thumb in the ear of the person with whom he is speaking, he is probably standing at the correct distance for personal distance.
_____ 7. Dr. Hall identified four distance zones used by Americans.
_____ 8. Personal distance would be appropriate for teachers and students.
_____ 9. Americans have continuous direct eye contact during communication.
_____ 10. Americans can use space to show power.

Vocabulary Words

You can frequently guess the meaning of a word by reading the sentences around it. Find the paragraph in the essay on pages 105–109 with the same number as the number in parentheses. Then find the word that fits the definition and write it in the blank.

Example:

(Paragraph 1) The study of space _____*proxemics*_____

(Paragraph 3) To fight _____

(Paragraph 8) To enter _____

(Paragraph 8) Close, in the same area _____

(Paragraph 8) Aggressive _____

(Paragraph 8) Distant emotionally _____

(Paragraph 9) Very, very good _____

(Paragraph 10) To avoid _____

Vocabulary Exercise

Fill in the blanks with vocabulary words listed on pages 104 and 110. The answers follow.

1. When you have a headache, it helps to rub your _____.

2. The dining room table was painted a shiny black. It has a beautiful _____ look.

3. The two boys were fighting and _____, rolling on the ground.

4. She is such a smooth dancer that she _____ across the floor like a skater.

5. I lost a lot of weight and now all my clothes are too big. They are _____ on me.

6. The sun was so hot that I almost fainted. I could _____ it. I didn't think I could take it.

7. He took the lady to a fancy restaurant and then to the theater. She felt like he treated her _____.

8. The men were _____ the sugar cane with their machetes.

9. It is not _____ to wear tennis shoes to the opera. The correct dress would be formal shoes.

10. I knew there was a surprise when my sister answered the door and she was _____

_____ and smiling.

1. temples 2. lacquered 3. wrestling 4. glides 5. baggy 6 scarcely bare 7. royally 8. slashing 9. appropriate 10. grinning

Word Forms

In English, the past participle of a verb can be used as an adjective. Choose the correct word form to fit into the following sentences. Write the part of speech at the end of each sentence (adjective or verb).

to penetrate, penetrated

1. The pen _____ the paper. (   )

2. The paper was _____. (   )

to avert, averted

1. We narrowly_____ an accident. (   )

2. A terrible accident was narrowly_____. (   )

to wrestle, wrestled

1. He _____ the book out of my hand. (   )

2. The book was _____ out of my hand. (   )

to tense, tensed

1. The athlete _____ his muscles. (   )

2. His muscles were _____. (   )

to dominate, dominated

1. The Olympics were _____ by Germany. (   )

2. Germany _____ the Olympics. (   )

Exercise on Space

Objective: To experience spatial differences in different cultures.

Using string or ribbons to measure the distances, role play the following situations as Hall says Americans would.

INTIMATE DISTANCE

You are in an extremely crowded elevator with a group of Americans. You do not know them. You don't want any problems.

SOCIAL DISTANCE

You are engineers working on separate projects in the same room.

PERSONAL DISTANCE

You are close friends and/or husbands and wives at a cocktail party.

Now choose one culture in your group and do the same situation as would members of that culture.

Is your culture's attitude toward hospitality closer to the American attitude or the Arab attitude? Discuss your answers with a partner.

Observation Exercise

Observe Americans and write a description of your observation. Use the following format; however, you may add any information that you feel is important. Make at least two observations.

FORMAT
1. Time behavior was observed.
2. Place behavior was observed.
3. Your relationship to the situation.
4. How many people are involved.

5. Draw a diagram of where each person was.
6. What was the distance between them?
7. Was this constant?
8. How long did you observe the behavior?
9. Based on the reading, what do you think their relationship is?
10. Would you have a different opinion if they were people from your culture?

Worksheet: My House

On the back of this page, sketch the floor plan of your parents' house (or the house in which you grew up). Include names of rooms, important furniture, and locations of doors. Be prepared to explain the diagram to your group, and to discuss the following questions.

How many people live in this home?

Which doors are usually left open?

Which doors are usually left closed? Which are locked and when are they locked?

Does (did) each child have his or her own room?

Where are visitors entertained? Where do visitors sleep?

Are any spaces primarily the territory of one family member? Which ones? Which family members do these spaces belong to?

How are the outer boundaries of the home marked? (Is there a yard? A courtyard which is shared with other homes? Is there a fence?)

Explain your diagram with a partner. Do the diagrams reflect cultural values? If so, how?

The Following Books Have More Information
about Cultural Proxemics.

Hall, Edward T.,   *The Hidden Dimension.* New York: Doubleday and Company, 1966. **A classic.**
———.   *The Silent Language.* New York: Doubleday and Company, 1959. **A classic classic.**

The Following Have More Information about Vietnam.

Fitzgerald, Frances,   *Fire in the Lake.* Boston, MA: Little, Brown & Co., 1972. **Pulitzer Prize winning portrayal of the villages and cities of Vietnam as if through Vietnamese eyes.**
Matthews, Ellen,   *Culture Clash.* Yarmouth, ME: Intercultural Press, 1982. **A portrait of an American family and the Vietnamese refugee family that they sponsored. Presents a picture of the problems and victories of each.**
Normand, Sully and Marjorie Weiner,   *We the Vietnamese—Voices from Vietnam.* New York, Washington, and London: Praeger Publishers, 1971. **A collection of essays by Vietnamese about Vietnamese.**
Films: "The Killing Fields" (although about Cambodia, gives a feel of the special horror of the war in Southeast Asia and the unique relationship between the Southeast Asians and the Westerners).

Chapter 10

Najwa Al-Akhras

The last student we will meet is Najwa Al-Akhras from Damascus, Syria. Her story begins as she wakes in the morning, and then proceeds through a typical day at the university. Notice the culture bumps that she has with the people around her and notice, in particular, the difference in orientation toward time that she has.

Non-English Words that Appear in the Reading "Najwa Al-Akhras: Syria"

koh'l – a black substance used by many women in the Middle East to outline their eyes
Koran – the holy book in the religion of Islam
henna – a natural, red dye used by many women in the Middle East
mlaya – a white, waist-length head covering worn by women in Syria when they pray
Marhaba – hello
Ahlane, ahlane – extended greetings

NAJWA AL-AKHRAS: SYRIA

Short with shoulder-length, thick, *hennaed* hair, she has creamy white skin and large, dark brown eyes. She **frets** about her inclination toward **plumpness,** especially now in the United States where the national obsession with thinness is contrary to the Middle Eastern appreciation of beauty. She dresses according to Paris styles that will not arrive in the United States for some time, always making her seem a bit out of place among the American coeds on campus.

She is at times amused at the simple mindedness of the Americans around her, as when her American roommate stated,

"That's not real gold. It can't be, its too bright,"

as she fingered the 24-carat gold necklaces (one with a copy of a page from the *Koran*) and the bracelets that Najwa always wears. At other times she is amazed at their worldiness, as when the same roommate casually offered her **birth control pills.**

Born in Damascus, Syria, she grew up in an upper-class family where East and West **fused** in the person of her father, Dr. Abdullah Al-Akhras. Raised in a home where the family spoke French in addition to their native Arabic, and traveled yearly to Europe, she is accustomed to cultural differences. Yet her deepest identity is rooted in her role as an Al-Akhras and in the Islamic teachings of her mother and grandmother.

Now she sometimes wakes before dawn and in her mind's eye sees her grandmother as she **knelt** with Najwa and her two sisters on the cold tile floor of their bedroom in Damascus, the old woman's grey hair peeping from beneath her *mlaya* as she kept an eye on her three granddaughters. At those moments, her chest **constricting,** Najwa recalls the faces of the females that surrounded her from birth, her sisters, her mother, her cousins next door, her aunts:

Going to afternoon tea in the old Damascus coffee house—elegant with its hand-painted tiles, imported chandeliers, and rich damask-covered sofas overlooking the slow moving brown Barada River that divides Damascus. The doe-eyed women held paper thin china cups of hot fragrant mint or ceylon tea as they gossiped, eyed **potential** mates for their sons, commented on the changing bodies of the girls as they matured. These women were sure of their roles in life, some happier than others, but none questioning the cycle of life Allah **ordained**—child, woman, wife, mother, mother-in-law, grandmother.

The family going to Cyprus on holiday, her older brother accompanying her and her sisters into the European shops lining the sparkling sea.

She and her friends gathering in the bedroom where amidst endless **giggling,** they tried on one another's clothes and jewelry and **speculated** on their future husbands and secret crushes.

But always underlying this, Najwa had had an unspoken yearning for something more, something different.

This morning as she lay in her bed, facing another day without the closeness and warmth that had enveloped her since birth, she questioned her own wisdom in convincing her father to allow her to study for a Master's degree in the United States and sensed she had lost something, an innocence, that could never be **retrieved.**

As she fully wakes, these feelings sink to a semiconscious level and she begins her day. She decides to dress casually "like an American." After dressing, she clasps on all her gold necklaces, snaps two gold bracelets around her wrist, dangles **filigreed** gold earrings from her ears, applies a third coat of mascara to her dark lashes and outlines her eyes in black *kho'l*. She finishes with a spray of perfume, runs a comb through her hair and she is ready. She bypasses the cafeteria in favor of a cup of coffee from the machine in the English building. Even though the liquid in the paper cup is a sickly tasting imitation of real coffee, she prefers to have it with Nadia and Samira. It reminds her of drinking the thick, sweet Turkish coffee with her family in the mornings. Carefully noting what they are wearing, she kisses each girl on each cheek,

"*Marhaba.*"
"*Ahlane, ahlane.*"
"How are you?"
"Fine."
"How did you sleep?"
"Fine. How are you?"
"Thanks be to God."
"How was the movie last night?"
"It was good."
"I talked with my family this morning."
"How are they?"
"Thanks be to God, but my grandfather is sick again."
"Oh, I'm sorry. I hope he is better."
"Is he in the hospital?"
"No, he's at home."
"Oh, that's good."
"I hope he is better."

The girls sit close and Samira touches Nadia's arm, both understanding that her grandfather's illness will affect Nadia's **disposition** that day and the following days.

"Well, you must study hard and not think too much about it."

"Yes, I'm trying."

"Uh, oh, it's 9:10. We're late."

"Let's go."

Najwa waves good-bye to her friends, knocks on the door of the class, opens it and steps inside,

"Excuse me please, Miss Joy."

As she sits down, she wonders once again at the American insistence on everything being at a certain time. She really tries to be on time and feels satisfied that she usually isn't late more than once a week and then always for a good reason. Like today when she had to be with Nadia who needed her. She hands in her homework, carefully written out last night, her Arabic/English dictionary close at hand. While handing in her paper, she looks at the other students' homework papers to see how they are doing.

Najwa likes Miss Joy and frequently raises her hand to answer or ask questions. She is also very curious about her teacher; she wonders what it is like to live alone in an apartment and whether Miss Joy thinks about getting married or is worried that at her age she might not find a suitable husband and have children.

She remembered her astonishment when another teacher had told Nadia that asking a teacher if she was married and had children was not an appropriate question in America. Nadia and her friends had decided, rather reluctantly, that maybe Americans didn't love children the way they did. Even in her desire for "something more in life," Najwa had never doubted that one day she would marry and have children but, of course, be more modern than her mother.

She ate lunch with Nadia (who was withdrawn), Samira, and Luz Maria. It still felt strange to eat lunch at 12:00 and then to rush back to class in only one hour. Back home, lunch had been at 2:00, with all the family present and a nap afterwards. Later her father went back to work while she and her sisters went shopping and then spent four to five hours doing homework. She'd been amazed at the American students' complaining about all the work they had to do; it was actually very light compared to the coursework she had carried at the University of Damascus.

At 4:00, she thanked the teacher for class and said good-bye to her classmates. She went to the library where Nadia, Samira, Phi, and she spent three hours studying until time for dinner. After dinner, she wrote letters to her parents, her sisters, her brother studying in Rome, and finally fell into bed to dream a confusing mixture of the streets of Damascus, English verbs, and her grandmother.

Vocabulary Words

1. **frets**—worries
2. **plumpness**—overweight
3. **birth control pills**—pills used to keep from getting pregnant
4. **fused**—came together
5. **deference**—respect
6. **knelt**—to be on the floor on one's knees

 7. **constricting**—getting tight
 8. **potential**—possible
 9. **ordained**—ordered
10. **giggling**—laughing
11. **speculated**—guessed
12. **yearning**—desire
13. **retrieved**—got back
14. **filigreed**—very delicate, lacy metalwork
15. **disposition**—mood

Discussion Questions

In small groups discuss the following questions. Be prepared to share your discussion with the class.

1. Where is Najwa in the adjustment cycle? Give specific examples to explain your answers. (See page 19.)

2. What did you learn about women in Syrian culture from this reading?

3. How does Najwa feel about Miss Joy? How do you suppose Miss Joy feels about Najwa?

4. Analyze the cultural influence in the conversation on page 119 between Najwa, Nadia and Samira. Can you identify the pattern of communication discussed on page 78?

TIME AND TIME AGAIN

Najwa, like most foreigners in the United States, has quickly learned that time is very important to Americans. She has learned some superficial "rules" about time and life in the United States. However, what she has not learned are the deeply held beliefs about time that permeate American culture, for time is a cultural concept. It is defined by the people of a culture and fits their ideas of what is good and bad, of what is real and unreal. We can intellectually understand that time is different for different peoples but it is very difficult to emotionally tolerate people behaving about time in a way that differs from our own behavior. (1)

Clock Time

John Horton in his article "Time and Cool People" characterizes time in industrialized societies as "clock time." It is an external regulator of the lives of the people. It divides the day and night into precise units or blocks. It is like a tangible product that we can save, waste, hold, or lose (Samover and Porter, pp. 90–91). It is also viewed as being linear and as having a past, present, and future. It puts a heavy emphasis on the future. It is impersonal and rational (Ibid, p. 15). An example of this is the perception of time in middle-class America, in which the present is seen as being only a "way station" between the future and the past. Since the present is not considered to be very important, there is little emphasis placed on the immediacy of one's experience. People in industrialized societies tend to live for the future and not to live in the present. (2)

Felt Time

In contrast, some cultures place more emphasis on the present and on what is called "felt time." For example, Japanese Zen sees time like a pool of water in which things happen: there is no linear past, present, or future. Things are "felt" or experienced in the present and that is the only reality. Both the Navajo and Sioux Indians place very little emphasis on the future. The Sioux language does not even have words for time, late, or waiting.* (Richard E. Porter, p. 15.) (3)

Quickly or Slowly

Just as concepts of time differ from one culture to another, so does the "time" of speaking. Some cultures place a great importance on responding rapidly, while others believe that fast talkers are foolish or suspicious. Our culture teaches us to speak fast or slowly (Richard E. Porter, p. 16). For example, Japanese need a longer period of time to respond to a question asked in the classroom, approximately 15 seconds as opposed to the American pattern of 7 seconds. This differs significantly from Latin American, American, and Middle Eastern patterns. In all three of these cultures, there is a pattern of speaking as quickly as possible. Indeed, the ability to "think on one's feet" is highly

*Adapted from L. A. Samovar and R. E. Porter, eds., *"Time," Intercultural Communication, A Reader.* Belmont, CA: Wadsworth, 1972.

valued in all three cultures. However, the Japanese place great value on not offending anyone. Therefore, they like to think carefully about what they say before uttering it. (4)

The Use of Time

Different cultures will also use time differently. Americans try to crowd as many activities into an hour as possible. This comes from the emphasis on competition in American culture. The drive to compete and achieve demands that one use time as fully as possible. In cultures where there is less emphasis on competition, people are able to let time "fill itself," or place more emphasis on quality of actions rather than quantity of actions. Americans, in contrast, need to constantly do something "useful." For example, many will use the time while they are driving to learn a new language or dictate letters, rather than using the time for meditation or looking at the landscape (5).

Doing Versus Being Versus Being in Becoming

As Stewart points out in *American Cultural Patterns*, in American culture, "doing" is pervasive. He gives the example of a typical greeting, "How are you doing?" This emphasis on "doing" leads to the idea that visible achievements which can be measured are the only desirable outcome of one's efforts. This contrasts with two forms of activity that dominate in some non-Western cultures, "being" and "being in becoming." In cultures where these activities are dominant, there is great respect paid to people who contemplate and meditate. Emphasis is placed on the total person, with an attempt to balance all aspects of the individual, in contrast to the "doing" society which places emphasis on measurable actions. (6)

By placing an emphasis on the future and on "doing," Americans have what Stewart calls "effort-optimism." Thus, through one's effort or hard work one will achieve one's ambitions. No goal is too remote, no obstacle is too difficult, for the individual who has the will and the determination and who expends the effort. Hard work is rewarded by success. The converse also holds. Failure means the individual did not try hard enough, is lazy, or is worthless. These harsh evaluations may be moderated, since one can have bad luck (Stewart, pp. 38–39). (7)

Monochronic Versus Polychronic Time

Another difference between cultures concerns monochronic and polychronic time. Monochronic cultures (i.e., American) do one thing at a time and place a great emphasis on taking turns, while polychronic cultures can do several things at one time and are comfortable doing many things at once. (8)

Conclusion

Time, far from being merely a measure of minutes and hours, is a fundamental part of our lives influencing what we do, how we do it, and with whom we do it. It changes across cultures just as drastically as languages and behaviors do. And because of this, in order to understand the people of a culture, it is important to understand their orientation to time. (9)

Comprehension Questions

Put an F by those statements that are false and a T by those that are true. Rewrite the false statements so that they are true.

_____ 1. Different cultures have different orientations toward time.

_____ 2. In industrialized societies, time is "felt time."

_____ 3. In societies that have "clock time," time is tangible.

_____ 4. Japanese need approximately three seconds more to respond to a question than do Westerners.

_____ 5. Americans try to crowd as many activities as possible into an hour.

_____ 6. Visible measurable achievements are generally the only ones with value in American culture.

_____ 7. Being on time is merely a habit with most Americans and has no deeper meaning.

_____ 8. Competition in American culture contributes to the American emphasis on doing as many things as possible in an hour.

_____ 9. American culture places more emphasis on the present than most cultures.

_____ 10. Monochronic cultures do many things at the same time.

Vocabulary Words

You can frequently guess the meaning of a word by reading the sentences around it. Find the paragraph in the essay on pages 121–124 with the same number as the number in the parentheses. Then find the word that fits the definition and write it in the blank.

Example:

(Paragraph 1) To go throughout _____*permeate*_____

(Paragraph 1) To put up with, to bear _____

(Paragraph 2) Concrete, real _____

(Paragraph 4) To say _____

(Paragraph 5) A need, a desire _____

(Paragraph 5) Thinking deeply and peacefully _____

(Paragraph 5) Scenery _____

(Paragraph 6) Everywhere _____

(Paragraph 6) To think _____

(Paragraph 7) Distant _____

(Paragraph 7) Opposite _____

(Paragraph 7) Hard _____

Vocabulary Exercise

Fill in the blanks with vocabulary words listed on pages 120 and 121. The answers follow.

1. The little girls were laughing and _____ during the class.

2. The plane landed on a _____ island in the Pacific that had no communication with the mainland.

3. I spent hundreds of dollars on the gift. It was a large _____.

4. The woman _____ on her knees to pray in the church.

5. The heat _____ the two metal bars together.

6. The mother worries and _____ when her baby has a fever.

7. They plant flowers and plants in order to create a beautiful _____.

8. He spoke such _____ words that the girl started crying.

9. The dog ran and _____ the stick that I threw.

10. He was so homesick. He had a strong _____ to see his family again.

1. giggling 2. remote 3. expenditure 4. knelt 5. fused 6. frets 7. landscape 8. harsh 9. retrieved 10. yearning

Word Forms

In English, a noun can be formed by adding a suffix to the verb form. In this exercise, the suffixes are -ion, -ance, or -ure. Choose the correct word form to fit into the following sentences. Write the part of speech at the end of each sentence (noun or verb).

Example:
to tolerate, toleration

1. *I refuse _____to tolerate_____ his bad behavior. (verb)*

2. *Your _____toleration_____ of his bad behavior only encouraged it. (noun)*

to permeate, permeatation

1. The water _____ the carpet. (   )

2. The carpet has a water _____. (   )

to utter, utterances

1. Those _____ cannot be called speech. (   )

2. The monkey_____ some sounds. (   )

to meditate, meditation

1. She _____ for several hours. (   )

2. She does _____ every day. (   )

to contemplate, contemplation

1. I _____ my options for several days. (   )

2. After much _____, I made my decision. (   )

to expend, expenditure

1. The city _____ all its money. (   )

2. The _____ of all the money broke the city. (   )

Draw time

Exercises

In groups of five to seven people (preferably from differing cultures), show and discuss your drawings of time. Note how they fit images of time as discussed in the article. Are they linear? Are they cyclical? Do they represent clock time? Do they represent felt time? Did you draw time in the United States? If so, would time be drawn the same way for your culture?

In groups of five to seven people (preferably from differing cultures), discuss the following definition which appeared in a newspaper.

> **Leisure counselor**—a professional advisor whose job it is to help people develop or find out what they really like to do for pleasure in their free time.

Is the preceding a *real* job description in the United States? Why or why not? Would this job exist in your culture? Why or why not? What do you suppose the word *workaholic* means?

In your groups discuss the following article which appeared in a newspaper.

> A judge ordered a dentist to pay his patient $115. The dentist had to pay the money because the patient had to wait for more than one hour past his appointed time. The judge said, "When somebody makes an appointment, they are entitled to that time."

Would this happen in your culture? Why or why not?

In your group, list as many expressions as you can in English in which the word *time* exists. What does this exercise reveal about Americans' attitude toward time? Think about expressions in your language. Are they concerned with time? If not, what are they concerned with?

Outside Activity

Ask five Americans what time it is. Notice what their answers are *exactly*. What do their answers reveal about their attitude about time?

THE FOLLOWING BOOKS HAVE MORE INFORMATION ABOUT CULTURAL TIME.

CASS, PIERRE, *Training for the Cross Cultural Mind.* Washington, DC: Society for Intercultural Education, Training and Research, 1980.
HALL, EDWARD T., *Beyond Culture.* New York: Anchor Press, 1976.
    . *The Dance of Life: The Other Dimension of Time.* New York: Doubleday/ Anchor Press, 1983.

SAMOVAR, LARRY A. and RICHARD E. PORTER, *Intercultural Communication: A Reader. Belmont, CA: Wadsworth Publishing Company, Inc., 1972.* Chapters on time across cultures.

THE FOLLOWING HAVE MORE INFORMATION ABOUT SYRIA.

FERNEA, ELIZABETH, *Guests of the Sheik,* London: Hale, 1968.
———, and BASIMA QATLAN BEZIRGAN, *Middle Eastern Muslim Women Speak.* Austin: University of Texas Press, 1984.
———, *Women and Family in the Middle East: New Voices of Change.* University of Texas Press, Austin, 1985. These three books by Fernea represent Middle Eastern women accurately. She also has a film series on women in the Middle East that is excellent.
HITTI, PHILIP K., *History of Syria, Including Lebanon and Palestine.* 2nd ed. London and New York: Macmillan Co., 1957. This is about history and politics in Syria.

Chapter 11

The Party

The final chapter finds all of the students having a party to celebrate the end of the semester at the home of the teacher, Joy Taylor. As in the first chapter, it is told from the point of view of the teacher. Has her point of view about the students changed? If so, in what way? How is the relationship between the students different? Lastly, notice how Joy represents American culture.

THE PARTY

"Damn."

Joy Taylor sucked the blood from the small cut on her thumb. She picked up the tomato slices and arranged them on a plate.

"O.K., what else? I think that's it. Now to get me ready."

As she sat in front of the mirror putting on her makeup, she noticed the dark circles under her eyes.

"Jeez, I'm tired after grading those finals. Well, at least I didn't have to take them. My poor students. They did pretty good though."

The doorbell rang and she glanced at her watch.

"7:25—they're early."

She quickly brushed rouge on her cheeks.

She opened the door and saw a huge bouquet of purple flowers held by Najwa. Phi and Luz Maria stood on each side of her.

"Oh how beautiful! Let me put them in here. Come on in. Have a seat. Make yourselves comfortable. Excuse me just a moment while I finish up. There are Cokes and other drinks on the table. The punch in the blue bowl has alcohol in it. The other doesn't. Help yourselves."

She **scampered** back to the bathroom to run a comb through her hair. As she came out, Luz Maria was opening the door and Abdul Aziz and Brian came in. The bell rang again as Nobuhito and Yuko arrived bringing Li Li with them. Soon the apartment was filled with people and the air was filled with laughter and the smell of food. Dishes covered the table—Luz Maria's "empanadas," Najwa's "upside down," Abdul Aziz's "capsa," Brian's tuna casserole, Yuko's "sushi," Li Li's dumplings, and Phi's spring rolls. Joy **absentmindedly nibbled** at a spring roll as she looked at her students spread out in the living room. She thought about what they had gone through during the semester—Luz Maria's **disappointment** with her roommate and Najwa's **bewilderment** when Joy had **reprimanded** her for being late. Her eye fell on Li Li sitting alone in a chair in the corner. She had become more and more isolated. Joy made a mental note to encourage her to volunteer to help with the orientation for new students. Maybe that would help.

Brian sat next to Nobuhito. Nobuhito had certainly **made a turnaround,** so melancholy until that picnic they had had at the beach. And who would have thought that he and Brian would have formed such a close friendship? But then, they both were business oriented. Brian had even gone out to his house several times for dinner.

Abdul Aziz walked over and settled on the **ottoman** next to Brian. Joy never had known just what had happened between the two boys. But the tension had grown worse and worse until it **came to a head** several weeks ago in class. Strange that it had been quiet, shy Phi who had intervened on that day when Abdul Aziz stood up to give a report on American families. Joy could still recall his words,

"The difference between Saudi fathers and American fathers is very great. Saudi fathers have responsibility for their sons and always help them and give them advice. But American fathers don't care for their sons, even talking about sex in front of them. Even they get divorced and leave their sons. I hate American fathers."

Brian exploded,

"Man, you don't know what you're talking about. If you hate it so bad, why the hell don't you just go back?"

"I wish to go now if I could."

*Their faces **contorted** and they moved toward one another, voices louder and louder.*

"Anyhow if you're so great, how come you make your women wear those stupid veils? Sure you don't have divorce—you can have as many women as you want," Brian snorted.

"You don't respect women. Look at the pictures of women with no clothes. Americans don't know how . . ."

"Stop!"

*Everyone turned in shock to look at Phi, standing by her desk with her hands **clenched at** her sides. Tears streamed down her face. She stood silent, breathing deeply.*

"Don't you understand? We must listen. We must listen. We must stop fighting. We lose everything when we fight. Please. . . ."

She sank into her chair.

Joy smiled recalling Brian and Abdul Aziz awkwardly apologizing to one another, to her, and to their classmates on the following day.

The **blare** of rock music brought her back to the party. Luz Maria moved from the stereo and grabbed Abdul Aziz to dance. She moved prettily from one side to the other while Abdul Aziz did his best to follow. Brian took Phi's hand to dance but she shook her head and giggled. Finally Najwa danced spiritedly with him. Everyone applauded as Nobuhito and Yuko got on the floor. Joy went over to Phi and Li Li,

"Come on, girls—let's dance."

Thirty minutes later, Alfredo arrived with several bottles of rum just in time to see his entire class and his teacher wildly dancing. He quickly joined in as the group formed a circle and began to clap and shout,

"Colombia"

Luz Maria moved to the center of the circle and danced while her classmates cheered.

"Saudi Arabia"

Abdul Aziz entered the center to the cheers of the others.

"Syria"

Najwa skillfully waved her arms in an approximation of Arabic dancing to American music.

"Japan"

To the delight of the others, Nobuhito and Yuko danced slowly and formally inside the circle.

"Vietnam"

And Phi took center stage.

"Venezuela"

Squeals and laughter accompanied Alfredo as he tried to drag at least three girls into the center with him.

"United States"

And Brian and Joy pranced around the onlookers.

"China"

Everyone pulled Li Li into the center. After standing still for a moment, a smile spread over her face and she moved gracefully. The dancers then formed **a congo line** and snaked their way through the apartment amid much laughter, finally collapsing on sofas and the carpet.

"Come on—let's eat."

It was Brian who had been hungrily eyeing the table. The noise level died down as the food was consumed and Joy thought about the dance. A similar version was danced at each end-of-the-semester party—a primal celebration and affirmation of their cultural diversity. Lines from an old song ran through her mind,

> *When true simplicity is gained*
> *To bow or to bend*
> *We shan't be ashamed*
> *To turn, turn*
> *Will be our delight*
> *Till by turning, turning*
> *We come round right*

How like that song we are, turning around one another until we turn into ourselves.

The group settled down listening to music and visiting among themselves. Joy turned the lights out and only the Christmas tree lights shone on their faces. A hush fell over the contented group. The song kept playing through her mind

> **Tis** *a gift to be simple*
> **Tis** *a gift to be free*
> **Tis** *a gift to come round*
> *Where we ought to be*
> *And when we find ourselves*
> *In the place just right*
> **T'will** *be in the valley of love and delight.*

Joy smiled and asked,
"Anybody for coffee?"

Vocabulary Words

1. **disappointment**—disillusionment
2. **bewildered**—puzzled, confused
3. **reprimanded**—scolded
4. **made a turnaround**—got better
5. **ottoman**—foot stool
6. **came to a head**—climaxed
7. **contorted**—grimaced, distorted
8. **clenched**—tightly closed

9. **blare**—loudly playing
10. **scampered**—went quickly
11. **absentmindedly nibbled**—ate in small bites without thinking
12. **congo line**—people dancing one behind the other
13. **primal**—primitive
14. **t'will**—it will
15. **tis**—it is

Discussion Questions

In small groups, discuss the following questions. Be prepared to share your discussion with the class.

1. How have the students in Joy's class changed during the semester? How have you changed during the semester?

2. Why did Phi shout during the argument between Brian and Abdul Aziz?

3. Why did the students dance in a circle and call out the names of the countries? Have you had a similar experience?

4. Explain the significance of the song that ran through Joy's mind during the party.

FRIENDS, TEACHERS, AND OTHER RELATIONS

Human relationships are enormously complicated. They are formed in a complex of individual, cultural, and universal influences. There is a constantly changing interplay among all of these influences in the relationships among Alfredo, Luz Maria, Phi, Abdul Aziz, Najwa, Brian, Miss Joy, Nobuhito, and Li Li. In examining the relationships within the class, several things become apparent. All of them have concepts of certain relationships, i.e., friendship. Furthermore, they all have assumptions of how people within these relationships should behave with one another. When their expectations are met, the other individual is characterized as "nice," "respectful," "caring," "friendly," and so on. If we ask where their assumptions came from, we discover that many of them are culturally based and have been refined by that particular individual's personality and life experience. The individual influence is seen in the relationship between Brian and Nobuhito who, although from dramatically different cultures, base a friendship on an individual interest in business. (1)

Cultural Values, Universal Concepts, and Universal Relationships

It is the interaction between three elements that give any culture its distinctive character. These three elements are (1) the particular values that receive a great deal of emphasis within a particular culture or *cultural values*, (2) concepts common to all cultures or *universal concepts*, and (3) relationships common in all cultures or *universal relationships*. (2)

American Individualism in Relationships

These cultural patterns manifest themselves in a thousand ways in American culture and subtly change from one individual to another. That a value receives emphasis in American culture does not mean that all Americans behave in the prescribed way. In fact, some will behave in the opposite way—simply because it is emphasized. Some will have not learned it at all. And each American will add his or her individual style to the behavior. Yet, it is possible to trace cultural patterns. In Stewart's work, *American Cultural Patterns,* he lists numerous cultural values. We examine only those of independence or self-motivation, fragmentation, equality, informality, and covert authority, all of which can be loosely grouped under the heading of individualism. We will see how these cultural values are manifested in the universal concepts of respect, love or caring, and helping. We will look at this interaction in relationships between students and teacher, between men and women, and among friends and discover how Americans evaluate the quality of each of these relationships. (3)

Independence and Self-motivation

Stewart writes that,

> Coming out of the past are several values that are tremendously important to Americans emotionally. One is self-reliance. This value is seen in the American's desire for autonomy, personal growth and most importantly, independence. By the same token, Americans try very hard not to be placed in a position of dependence. Self-reliance as it is seen in American culture cannot be translated into many other cultures. For example, it translates into Spanish as "independence" and suggests political and social freedom while in American culture it suggests that the Self is the sole factor. The Latin, with his strong

attachment to family and immediate group, does not dislike dependence as does the American. And for the Chinese, dependence is desirable because it strengthens relationships between people. Chinese parents, for example, take pride in being dependent on their children. . . . Unlike some other societies, American culture doesn't place much importance on where one is born, one's family or politics. Destiny and origin are not important; self-definition is determined by personal achievement. Motivation is based in the individual. He chooses his own goals and then decides how to reach them. (4) (Stewart, p. 72)

Independence and Self-motivation in American Friendships

Kathy was uncomfortable with Luz Maria talking about her problems and tried to help her by suggesting that she see a counselor. In this way, she "saved" Luz Maria's face by helping maintain her independence. She was reluctant to get involved; getting involved for Americans means that they are taking away someone's independence and thus "crippling" them. Americans, in order to show caring for one another, try to help one another maintain their independence. (5)

The American emphasis on self-motivation is in direct contrast with Alfredo who depended on his family name and his contacts and was very comfortable in doing so. An American might use contacts but there would also be an emphasis on doing it "myself." Li Li expected Brian and Gabriela to help her with her English. Gabriela's advice to get out and get involved was an example of the necessity to be self-motivated in American culture. (6)

Independence and Self-motivation in American Male/Female Relationships

Luz Maria can trust Jorge completely and depend on him to tell her what to do. She feels as comfortable with her dependence on him as he does and he, in return, will depend on her completely in "female" matters. American romantic relationships usually provide more independence for both the male and female than would Luz Maria and Jorge's relationship. Brian's girlfriend, for example, would have to be far more independent since Brian simply could not be with her as much as Jorge was with Luz Maria. And Brian's mother had independently raised her children without their father. American culture had made it possible, if not easy, for her to be independent of a husband. (7)

Independence and Self-motivation in American Teacher/Student Relationships

Most of the students in Joy's class were accustomed to depending on teachers in the classroom. Yet, most American teachers try to inculcate a sense of independence in their students. Students have considerable freedom to decide what they would like to do, or they are expected to do independent research with little direct instruction. American teachers assume that students will do their work independently. American students will ask questions in the class when they do not understand a point, as opposed to many Asian students who will wait until the class is over. (8)

Fragmentation

With regard to fragmentation, Stewart says,

> Because an individual's value is based on achievement, Americans feel they are replaceable and are spurred on to even greater achievement. Because people are defined according to their achievement, Americans can fragment their own personality or that of another. . . . The generalized "friend" of Americans, standing for anyone from a passing acquaintance to a life-long intimate, is maintained according to activities. . . . Thus, Americans have friendships which originate "around work, children, or political opinions". . . . The various compartments of friendship are kept separate so that a friendship that is centered around the office does not intrude into the relations with friends who participate in recreational activities. . . . In circumstances where a foreigner might turn to a friend for help, support or solace, the American will tend to search for the professional, prefering to not inconvenience his friends." (Stewart, p. 54, 73) (9)

Fragmentation in American Friendships

This contrasts with intense friendship as experienced by Abdul Aziz, whose closest friends were his cousins and with whom he did everything; they went to school together, on vacation together, ate at one another's homes. However, Brian, whose suggestion to study with Abdul Aziz was typical of forming friendship based on common activities (they are both in the same class) reflects the American's social friendship. Americans are comfortable forming relationships for a semester's time and then gradually seeing less and less of one another, although it is possible for a longer lasting friendship to result. Luz Maria and Kathy form another contrast in cultural values about friendship. Luz Maria assumes that since she is living with Kathy that they will be friends and thus wants to do many other things with her such as study, and so on. Kathy can have a relationship with Luz Maria in which they are roommates only and do not share the other areas of their lives. (10)

Fragmentation in American Male/Female Relationships

Fragmentation versus role definition shows up in male/female relationships also. If we look at the relationship between men and women as it is seen in the characters of Alfredo and Luz Maria, we see a strong emphasis on identity in role. Men and women are considered to be very separate; men do "men" things and women do "women" things. So Alfredo can say "piropos" at a girl and in his doing so, he affirms his role as a man and confirms her role as a woman. He does both of them a favor by his act. Kathy, although she enjoys compliments, doesn't define herself as strongly in the role of female. And the American co-ed who "spit" at Alfredo's admiring glance was insulted because he had defined her by role "female" rather than by individual achievement. (11)

Fragmentation in American Teacher/Student Relationships

Phi, for whom a teacher is a teacher forever, inside the class or outside, defines teacher by role. Joy's behavior is strange in Phi's eyes. Joy doesn't play the "role" of a teacher, and outside of the class can even be a friend. At the end-of-semester party, she is completely separate from her role of teacher, dancing with the students. In other words, Joy "fragments" by being a teacher in the class and an individual outside the class. Joy evaluates her role as a teacher, not by a predefined "role" but by how her students perform. Her success depends on their success. (12)

Equality and Covert Authority

Of equality, Stewart writes,

> Running throughout the American's social relationships with others is the theme of equality. Each person is thought to have value because of his humanness. . . . Interpersonal relations are typically horizontal, conducted between presumed equals. . . . People are taught to conform, not through direct authority, but by indirect social coercion. These pressures are informal, not formal, because the American is assumed to be a free agent. Americans cooperate in society not by coercion and authority, but by persuasion. The threat of failure is powerful in making Americans cooperate. Authority when it must be used is masked. (Stewart, p. 50). (13)

Equality and Covert Authority in American Friendships

In contrast to American covert authority patterns, direct orders and suggestions are possible, even welcomed in many cultures. For example, Najwa and Samira both give lots of "advice" to Nadia directly. Nadia interprets this as evidence of their caring for her. This contrasts with Kathy's indirect suggestions to Luz Maria, which was her form of caring. (14)

Equality and Covert Authority in American Male/Female Relationships

For the American male and female, equality is frequently interpreted as "the same." Thus, there is an emphasis on men and women being defined (at least in the workplace) by achievement, not by male or female roles. This explains the teacher telling Nadia that it was inappropriate to ask a teacher if she is married and has children. For the American professional woman, the question implies that she is to be judged on her role as a woman rather than on her achievements. (15)

Equality and Covert Authority in American Teacher/Student Relationships

Students from cultures with more overt authority patterns frequently do not "see" the more subtle authority expressed by Americans. Thus, Alfredo could comfortably be late to class since the professor didn't express displeasure overtly. An American would know that the authority would be expressed merely by looking at the late arriving student as he came in the classroom. An astute American student would then know that he or she is in trouble and would probably go up after class to apologize for being tardy. Nor would Alfredo necessarily realize that Joy's comment about his lack of studying reflected a serious level of anger on her part—for her to even say anything meant that he was already in trouble. Both of these behaviors on the part of the teachers are manifestations of "covert authority." (16)

Informality

An area of frequent conflict for foreigners in the United States is informality about which Stewart says,

> Americans tend to treat other people with informality and directness. Foreign students in the United States frequently have difficulty with this quality until they get used to it. When Americans employ their direct, brusque manners in dealing with other peoples, they are likely to insult or confuse them. The flowery language, complex methods of address, and ritualistic manners found in other cultures reflect the social structure of the people. Whereas, the average American considers formality, style, and protocol as pompous or arrogant, these provide dependable expectations in other cultures. . . . He reaches a first-name basis readily and early in a relationship. (Stewart, p. 53) (17)

Informality in American Friendship and Teacher/Student Relationships

While informality permeates all American relationships, it is particularly noticeable to foreigners in friendship and teacher/student relationships. It is obvious in Luz Maria's and Kathy's speech patterns. Luz Maria uses a more formalized greeting in the morning while Kathy gives brief, to-the-point answers with no emphasis on formality. Abdul Aziz's formal greeting of Brian causes Brian's initial discomfort and it is Brian's lack of formal greeting of guests that causes Abdul Aziz's great discomfort. Likewise, Phi's perception of proper, formal behavior for a teacher contrasts with Joy's informal, breezy behavior in the class as well as her informal behavior with her students at the party. (18)

Conclusion

From informality to independence, Americans reflect their culture's beliefs in a myriad of ways in their interactions with everyone they meet. For the foreigner in the United States, an understanding of the dominant beliefs helps to make comprehensible American life. Studying cultural patterns is akin to studying the wind. We can never completely capture it; it remains forever invisible and yet its impact is always a part of our life experience. (19)

Comprehension Questions

Put an F by those statements that are false and a T by those that are true. Rewrite the false statements so that they are true.

_____ 1. A relationship is manifested by the interplay between cultural values, universal concepts, and universal relationships.

_____ 2. Individualism includes independence, self-motivation, fragmentation, equality, informality, and covert authority.

_____ 3. Arabs only have friends so they can use them.

_____ 4. Americans define themselves according to their roles.

_____ 5. Kathy didn't care about Luz Maria.

_____ 6. Joy was "fragmenting" when she danced with her students at the party.

_____ 7. Authority in American culture, when it must be used, is masked.

_____ 8. American teachers don't care if students come to class late.

_____ 9. Americans are usually very formal in their dealings with people.

_____ 10. All Americans are very individualistic.

Vocabulary Words

You can frequently guess the meaning of a word by reading the sentences around it. Find the paragraph in the essay on pages 135–141 with the same number as the number in the parentheses. Then find the word that fits the definition and write it in the blank

Example:

(Paragraph 1) Suppositions _____ *assumptions* _____

(Paragraph 1) Made more evident, more clear _____

(Paragraph 3) Models or guides _____

(Paragraph 3) Hidden _____

(Paragraph 4) In control of oneself _____

(Paragraph 4) In the same way _____

(Paragraph 5) To save from being embarrassed _____

(Paragraph 5) To take away one's independence _____

(Paragraph 8) To instill, to foster _____

(Paragraph 9) To be motivated to go farther _____

(Paragraph 11) To reinforce _____

(Paragraph 11) To say very angrily _____

(Paragraph 13) Assumed _____

(Paragraph 13) Hidden _____

(Paragraph 15) Unacceptable _____

(Paragraph 16) Open, obvious _____

(Paragraph 16) Clever _____

(Paragraph 17) Rough and short in manner _____

(Paragraph 17) Ornate, complex _____

(Paragraph 17) Ceremonial _____

(Paragraph 17) Self-important (in a negative sense) _____

(Paragraph 17) Acting superior to other people _____

(Paragraph 18) Informal _____

(Paragraph 19) Like _____

Vocabulary Exercise

Fill in the blanks with vocabulary words listed on pages 134, 135, and 142. The answers follow.

1. The cat likes to sleep on the _____ that is in front of my father's chair.

2. At the party the people wore costumes to hide their identity. Almost all of them

    were _____ .

3. The Chinese have an old saying that means to spare someone from embarassment.

    They say that they _____ .

4. The weight lifter _____ his face when he lifted the barbells. Sweat broke
    out in beads all over his face.

5. Parents try to teach their children to be polite. They try to _____ them
    with good manners.

6. Rabbit meat is like chicken. It is _____ to several white meats.

7. His real motive in calling was to borrow money although he pretended to offer his

    help. His motives were _____ .

8. My neighbors play their radio very loudly. I can't sleep because of the _____
    of the music.

9. The teacher _____ the students for talking during the class. He was very
    angry.

10. I wanted very much to go to California for vacation and felt a lot of _____
    when I could not go.

Word Forms

Let's review the word forms. In the following sentences, form a noun by adding a suffix to the verb form, form an adjective by using the past participle form of the verb, use the same verb form as a noun, add an -ly to an adjective to form an adverb. Write the part of speech at the end of the sentence (adjective, verb, noun, adverb).

Example:
to assume, assumption

1. *I _____assume_____ that he will be there. (verb)*

2. *The _____assumption_____ is that he will be there. (noun)*

to refine, refinement

1. That plant is where they_____ sugar. (   )

2. The _____ of sugar occurs in that plant. (   )

to pattern, pattern

1. They _____ the movie after his life. (   )

2. The _____ of his life was used in the movie. (   )

autonomous, autonomously

1. He lived _____. (   )

2. He was _____ in his life. (   )

to affirm, affirm

1. The truth has been _____. (   )

2. He _____ that that is what happened. (   )

to spit, spit

1. We saw _____ on the sidewalk. (   )

2. He_____on the sidewalk. (   )

to coerce, coercion

1. There is no _____ in the matter. (   )

2. He did not _____ her. (   )

to mask, mask

1. There is a _____ on his face. (   )

2. He _____ his identity. (   )

Exercises

1. Linda went to Africa as an ESL teacher in a small village. She was a good teacher and worked hard during the day. At night, she went dancing, even though she knew that the African teachers in that village never went dancing. *Which American characteristic influenced Linda to go dancing? What do you think that the Africans thought of her? If you were Linda's supervisor (an American), how would you handle this situation? You want to keep her on as a teacher—but as an effective teacher.*

2. Two men are running for mayor of a small city in the United States. They have exactly the same qualifications. Both are lawyers, were excellent students, are very personable except that Joe comes from a rich, prestigious family and Frank comes from a poor family with a number of problems, including alcoholism and a father who never kept a job. *Which one will probably win the election? Why?*

3. A student from Lebanon asked his foreign student advisor her opinion about a certain college. She really thought that the school was terrible. She said, "Well, if I were you, I would look for some schools in another city. You should probably check around a little bit more." *Is she an effective advisor? Why or why not?*

4. There are two friends—one from Iran, one from the United States. The American arrived at the airport one night and discovered that he had no money. He called his Iranian friend who came and picked him up. The next day, the American gave the Iranian friend a nice book with a note saying, "Thanks for picking me up." The Iranian was puzzled by his actions. He felt that as a friend he was obligated to pick him up. *Which American characteristic prompted the American to give the book?*

Worksheet

List five characteristics that you look for in a friend. Put the more important ones first.

1.

2.

3.

4.

5.

How many friends do you have?

What would cause you to break a friendship?

List five ways in which authority is shown in your culture, with the most important way shown first.

1.

2.

3.

4.

5.

Who has authority in your culture?

Discuss your answers in your groups.

Crossword Vocabulary Review

Using the vocabulary words listed on pages 90, 91, 94, 104, 110, 120, 121, 124, 125, 134, 135, and 142, fill in the blanks in the puzzle.

ACROSS
1. demonstrations
5. To enter
7. Distant emotionally
8. Mood
12. Foot stool
14. Ordered
16. Very loud

DOWN
1. Thinking deeply and peacefully
2. Hit on the face with an open palm
3. Like
4. To say very angrily
6. To stay temporarily
8. Hidden
10. Throbbing, beating
11. Long thin sticks used to cook meat over fire
13. Merge
15. Avoid

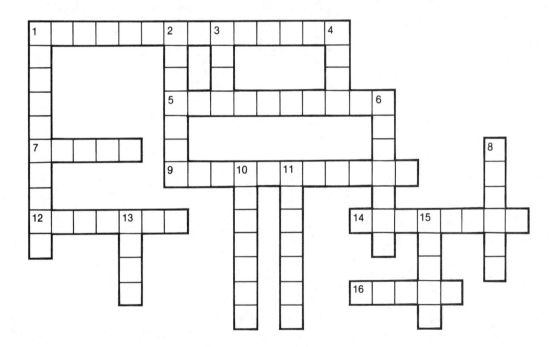

Answer to crossword puzzle on page 147.

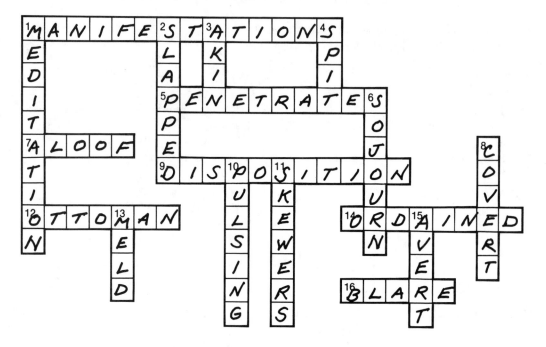

REVIEW QUESTIONS FOR CHAPTERS 6–11

1. Choose a culture bump that you have experienced. Tell whether it was positive, negative, or neutral. Analyze it using the ten steps in your book.
2. Compare and contrast the difference in the communication patterns of your culture and American culture.
3. Read the following two dialogues carefully and then analyze each one. Tell how American culture is reflected in them. Give specific examples of cultural values. Then rewrite the dialogue as it might be in your own culture.

Dialogue A

Mary: female lawyer. Joe: male accountant. They are friends but not close. They have met several times at parties. The following is a telephone conversation. Mary calls Joe.

> JOE: (*Telephone rings*)   Hello.
> MARY: Hello. Joe?
> JOE: Yes.
> MARY: This is Mary. Mary Jones. How are you?
> JOE: Fine, thanks. And you?
> MARY: Fine, thanks. Listen, Joe, the reason I'm calling is that I have several tickets for the Mozart concert next Friday night. And I thought that you might like to go together.
> JOE: I'd love to. Thanks for inviting me. Shall I pick you up?
> MARY: Sounds great. How about sevenish?
> JOE: Fine. I'll see you then. Thanks again.

Tell the specific American cultural values that are reflected in this dialogue. Rewrite the dialogue as it might happen in your culture.

Dialogue B

Betty and Sue are friends. They attend the university together. They have known one another for three years.

> BETTY: Hi Sue. How're you doing?
> SUE: Oh hi. Well OK I guess.
> BETTY: Doesn't sound OK. Are you sure you're OK?
> SUE: Well, the truth is I feel really depressed.
> BETTY: What about?

SUE: That grammar class is driving me crazy. I just can't seem to get it. You're great in there.

BETTY: Well, English has always been one of my best subjects. Listen, the English department has a tutoring program. Did you know about that?

SUE: No, I didn't. How do I get one?

BETTY: Well, you just go into the office and sign up. There's no charge or anything. I'll bet they could really help you.

SUE: Thanks a lot. I'm going to go over there right now.

Tell the specific American cultural values that are reflected in this dialogue. Rewrite the dialogue as it might happen in your culture.

4. Choose one of the characters from the book and pretend that he or she is your roommate. Write a letter from the point of view of an American to your family about your "new roommate."

FOR MORE INFORMATION:

CAMPBELL, JOSEPH with BILL MOYERS, *The Power of Myth.* New York: Doubleday, 1988.

SAMOVAR, LARRY A. and RICHARD PORTER, eds., "Beyond Cultural Identity: Reflections on Cultural and Multicultural Man," in *Intercultural Communication: A Reader.* Belmont, CA: Wadsworth Publishing, 1976, pp. 362–377.

FOR MORE INFORMATION ON AMERICAN CULTURE:

KEARNY, EDWARD N., MARY ANN KEARNY, and JO ANN CRANDALL, *The American Way: An Introduction to American Culture.* Englewood Cliffs, NJ: Prentice-Hall, Inc., 1984.

ROBERTSON, JAMES OLIVER, *American Myth American Reality.* New York: Hill & Wang, 1980.

STEWART, EDWARD C., *American Cultural Patterns: A Cross-Cultural Perspective.* Chicago: Intercultural Press, Inc., 1972.

Appendix

Outside Activity

A Traveling Cultural Circus

This activity provides for many advantages. It offers a chance for role play, and public speaking as well as informal speaking. The teacher can place more emphasis on writing and library skill development by requiring students to prepare background papers on their countries. This is also a useful exercise in evaluating how American sources present information about foreign countries.

For this project, the class is divided into groups of four to eight people. Each group is comprised of representatives of major geographical areas. For example, group 1 might consist of two Latin Americans, one Asian, two Middle Easterners, and one European. Each group would be assigned a cultural value that is universal, such as respect. Then each member would extrapolate the behaviors regarding respect in his or her own culture by using the culture bump method. It is more effective if all members apply the concept of respect between teachers and students in different cultures. The group prepares an "act" or presentation in which the concept of respect is demonstrated in each of the cultures represented by group members. They should take care to point out that the concept is constant across all cultures, while the manifestation of the concept may differ radically. Group members help one another to prepare each segment, thereby enabling all members to consider respect in their own cultures as well as those of each of their classmates in the group. The teacher can then contact local area schools (or other departments in a university or college) and arrange for a group to visit a different class each week. And each class would receive a different group each week. Thus, the foreign student groups form a "traveling cultural circus," moving from class to class (or school to school) on a weekly basis, while an individual class is visited by a different "act" each week.

Procedure for School Visits

1. All international students will have already visited an American high school or junior high school in order to observe before going out to present.
2. Either the week before or at the beginning of the week of visitation, the international students will get the following information to the host teacher: (a) a brief biography of each member of the team, (b) a brief summary of what the team will do

with each class, and (c) (optional) a brief background paper on the countries involved.

3. Each team will have a member that is responsible for contacting the teacher and arranging for the visit.
4. The emphasis is "experiential" during the visit.
5. Host teachers will have students prepared for the visit.

During the visit itself, the following is a suggested format:

1. Foreign students will come into the classroom, introduce themselves, and tell which country they come from. (five minutes)
2. They will divide the class into groups of four to five American students with two foreign students.
3. In the small groups, they will spend about five to eight minutes doing ice-breaking exercises, learning one another's names, asking questions about the topics, and letting the American students ask them questions about the topic.

At this point, they can stay in small groups or work with the class as a whole.

4. They spend about five minutes while the American students show them how they do whatever the topic concerns in the United States, for example, how students show respect to teachers.
5. Then they show the American students how this same thing is done in each of their cultures.
6. They ask the Americans to teach them how to do this like the Americans do it.
7. They then show the Americans how to do it as it is done in their cultures.

(Steps 6 and 7 are more effective if they are done in the original small groups.)

8. Then they will have a discussion about what they have done, how it is similar, how it is different, and how the behaviors reflect the values of each culture. The Americans can share what they have learned from their foreign resource people.

General Suggestions

1. Have the group members exchange phone numbers and addresses.
2. Allow time in class for groups to meet and encourage them to meet outside of class as often as possible, thereby forming a strong group identity.
3. *Always* have a group practice in class before going out on a visit. *Always* have groups report back to the entire class on their experience.
4. Encourage students to exhibit objects from their country or use national dress, if possible.

America Through Foreign Eyes

America Through Foreign Eyes is an exercise that enables the students to apply what they have learned in the units on American culture. In this exercise the students choose an area in American life which they will observe over a period of four to six weeks. During that time, they collect their observations and analyze them. They then make a report at the end of the six weeks in which they present their findings. This project requires no role play or cultural resourcing but does stress all the linguistic skill areas very emphatically.

In introducing this project, the teacher should present examples of the analysis to students. For example, the teacher can bring cartoons, newspaper articles, and so on to class and extrapolate the American values reflected in them.

The class should be broken into groups of five to seven people with as many different cultural backgrounds as possible being represented in each group.

Each group should then choose one of the following topics:

Comic strips
Newspaper articles
Commercials (on radio and/or TV)
TV shows
Music (should be specific, that is, Country Western, popular)

After choosing one of the topics, the group will decide which people within the group will do which tasks. Each person must monitor the topic and collect samples. The group will meet regularly to analyze the findings for the following information:

1. Evidence of American cultural values and/or behaviors
2. How the findings would be different or the same in each of the cultures in the group.

The group will then decide how to present a report on the findings. Some suggestions for presentations are:

1. Posters with cartoon or articles mounted on them, displayed during the presentation.
2. Tape recordings of commercials or music played during a presentation.
3. Video recordings of commercials or music played during a presentation.
4. Role playing of segments of shows or commercials.

In addition, each individual student should note differences in the way that the mixed-culture group operates as opposed to working in his or her own culture group.

Each student will submit one to two paragraphs describing this at the time of the presentation.

Groups should collect at least five to six samples in the chosen area.

Student Instructions

Working in groups, choose one of the following topics:

Comic strips
Newspaper articles
Commercials (on radio and TV)
TV shows
Music

After choosing one of the topics, assign people within your group to specific tasks. Each person must monitor the topic and collect samples. As a group, analyze the findings for the following points.

1. Evidence of American cultural values and/or behavior.
2. How the findings would be different or the same in each of the cultures represented in your groups.

The group will then decide how to present a report on its findings to the other classes.

Each individual student should note differences in the way that the mixed-culture group operates as opposed to working in his or her own regional group. Each individual student will submit one to two paragraphs describing this at the time of the group presentation.

Groups will meet together twice a week to complete the project.

Note: Monitoring the particular topic should begin immediately so that the group will have five to six samples of each topic.

Field Trip to a Grocery Store

The class visits a grocery store. Answer the following questions. After the field trip, have a group discussion of answers and impressions.

1. How many rows of canned goods are there?
2. How many rows of fresh vegetables and fruits are there?
3. How are the customers dressed? Is this different than it would be in your country?
4. Are there more men or women? Is this different than it would be in your country?

5. How do the customers pay? Is this different than it would be in your country?
6. What have you learned about American culture from this visit?

Field Trip to an Ethnic Neighborhood

The class visits an ethnic neighborhood (Hispanic, Asian, and so on). If possible, they eat in a restaurant, visit grocery stores as well as other kinds of stores, and any other types of establishments, such as movies, newspapers, banks. If there are students in the class from the ethnic background, use them as resource people.

They are given the following questions to answer. The teacher can change the questions to fit the local area.

Answer these questions on the same day of the visit. After the field trip, have a group discussion of answers and impressions.

1. What purpose does this neighborhood serve for the Americans in this city? What purpose does it serve for the ethnic community?
2. What are the differences between this grocery store and the grocery store visited earlier?
3. What are the differences between the restaurant and a "typical" American restaurant?
4. List sounds and smells that are different for you.

Sounds   Smells
1.   1.
2.   2.
3.   3.
4.   4.

5. Are there neighborhoods like this in your country?
6. What did you learn from this visit?

Model for Comparative Education Research Paper

Find the following information in a library for either your own country or one of your choice.

1. **Geography**
   Location
   Type of geography
   Climate
2. **Physical Infrastructure**
   Roads
   Shipping

Railroads
Electricity
Communication
   Telephone
   Newspapers
   TV, radio
3. **Political Organization**
   Type of government
   Branches of government
   Responsibility of government
4. **History**
5. **Economic Situation**
   Income (personal)
   Natural resources
   Industrialization
   Unemployment
6. **Population**
   Number of people
   Men versus women
   Birth rate
   Percentage of population below age of 15
7. **Educational System**
   Who is responsible for education?
   Physical diagram of system
   Tests between levels
   Requirements to be a teacher
   Percentage of males and females enrolled
   Compulsory attendance or not
   Private versus public schools

Festival Worksheet

1. Form groups of five to seven students from similar cultures.
2. Decide on a festival that is typical of your cultural background.
3. As a group, write a short description of the festival. Include a brief history of the festival and why it is celebrated. List customs associated with the festival: foods, special dress, music, dances, and so on. This description should be approximately two paragraphs long.
4. Plan your presentation, using the following steps:
   a. Decide on the activities you want to present, for example, music and dance. List the items you will need to present them. Decide who will be responsible for getting the items.
   b. Decide on foods you want to have. Decide who will be responsible for preparing the food.